WHAT'S IN A
CHINESE
CHARACTER

Tan Huay Peng

Marshall Cavendish
Editions

Other titles by Tan Huay Peng:
*Chinese Idioms Vol. 1& 2 • Chinese Radicals Vol. 1 & 2 • Hanyu Pinyin • Simplified Chinese Characters •
Fun with Chinese Characters Vol. 1-3*

© 1998 Federal Publications (S) Pte Ltd
© 2000 Times Media Private Limited
© 2005 Marshall Cavendish International (Asia) Private Limited

First published in 1998
Reprinted 1999, 2000, 2005, 2008

Based on *Fun with Chinese Characters Vol. 1-3*

Published by Marshall Cavendish Editions
An imprint of Marshall Cavendish International
1 New Industrial Road, Singapore 536196

Other Marshall Cavendish Offices:
Marshall Cavendish Ltd. 5th Foor, 32–38 Saffron Hill, London ECIN 8FH, UK • Marshall Cavendish Corporation. 99 White Plains Road, Tarrytown NY 10591-9001, USA • Marshall Cavendish International (Thailand) Co Ltd. 253 Asoke, 12th Flr, Sukhumvit 21 Road, Klongtoey Nua, Wattana, Bangkok 10110, Thailand • Marshall Cavendish (Malaysia) Sdn Bhd, Times Subang, Lot 46, Subang Hi-Tech Industrial Park, Batu Tiga, 40000 Shah Alam, Selangor Darul Ehsan, Malaysia

Marshall Cavendish is a trademark of Times Publishing Limited

National Library Board Singapore Cataloguing in Publication Data
Chen, Huoping.
What's in a Chinese character / Tan Huay Peng. – Singapore : Marshall Cavendish Editions, 2008.
p. cm.
ISBN-13 : 978-981-261-663-0
ISBN-10 : 981-261-663-2

1. Chinese characters. 2. Chinese language – Writing. I. Title.

PL1171
495.12 -- dc22   OCN238822822

Printed in Singapore by Fabulous Printers Pte Ltd

Preface

A Chinese script of one form or another has been in existence for over 5,000 years. Although it has continued to develop, the basic form of the writing was already established by 200 A.D. This makes it not only a very interesting aspect of Chinese life, but also one of mankind's greatest early achievements.

Chinese script consists of characters, which range from simple pictographic representations of objects, to complex compound characters. These are built up from root characters, or radicals. Of the 214 radicals, some can function independently as characters, and are then contracted when they appear in combination.

This set of cartoons illustrates how some of the radicals, and their associated characters, have evolved over the years. They make a useful introduction to the Chinese language and also provide a fascinating insight into the Chinese sense of humour.

Useful information is given on the types of stroke and stroke sequence, which will help those learning written Chinese. Also, the Chinese for numbers, days and months are provided in the Appendix.

Introduction

Historical Background

The origins of Chinese script are shrouded in mystery, and various legends exist to explain its creation. One such legend tells how Cāng Jí 仓颉, a minister of the Emperor Huáng Dì 黄帝, observed the footprints of birds and animals. He noticed how each one was distinct and recognizable. Inspired by this, Cāng Jí drew pictures of objects, simplifying them by reducing the number of lines. These were the first pictographs, called xiàng xìng 象形 by the Han lexicographer Xǔ Shèn 许慎 (30 A.D.-124 A.D.)

Pictographs

Certain items could be represented very well by pictographs, for example: animals; plants; parts of the body etc. As the development of a particular character is traced, we can see that, over time, it tends to lose some of its resemblance to the original.

Examples of Pictographs

⊖	日	rì	sun		水	shuǐ	water
	月	yuè	moon		火	huǒ	fire
	山	shān	mountain		木	mù	wood
	虎	hǔ	tiger		羊	yáng	sheep
	象	xiàng	elephant		马	mǎ	horse
	犬	quǎn	dog		目	mù	eye
	耳	ěr	ear		手	shǒu	hand
	口	kǒu	mouth				

Ideographs

These are characters which represent abstract concepts. Xǔ Shèn called them zhǐ shì 指事

Examples of Ideographs

一 yī   one
二 èr   two
三 sān three

上 shàng up, above
下 xià   lower, below

Determinative-Phonetic Characters

As civilization grew, so did the demand for new characters. To this end, a new type of character was invented called determinative-phonetic, or xíng shēng 形声

These characters have a determinative part, to convey the meaning, and a phonetic part to show pronunciation.

Examples of Determinative-Phonetic Characters with a Similar Pronunciation

Determinative	Phonetic	Compound
水 shuǐ (water; abbrev. 氵)	+ 其 qǐ (his, her its this, that; originally winnowing basket, now 箕)	→ 淇 qí (the River Qi)
玉 yù (jade; abbrev. 王)	+ 其 qí	→ 琪 qí (a valuable white stone or gem)
木 mù (tree; wood)	+ 其 qí	→ 棋槃 qí (chinese chess)

This shows how words with the same pronunciation are written completely differently.
其 qí is always a phonetic when it appears in a compound word, although it can function as a character itself, meaning his, her, its etc.

Examples of Determinative-Phonetic Characters with a Similar Meaning

木 mù (wood) +
土 tǔ (earth; land; ground)

→ 杜 dù (the russet pear; to shut out;
to stop; to prevent)

木 mù (wood) +
反 fǎn (to turn over; to rebel; to turn back)

→ 板 bǎn (board; blocks for printing)

Every pictograph can be used as a phonetic, but only a few function as determinatives. This system of radicals was introduced to enable characters to be classified in a dictionary. By the time of the Ching Dynasty (1644 A.D - 1911 A.D.) the number of radicals had been reduced to its current level of 214.

Apart from the three major groups of characters already mentioned, there are also a few others.

Associative compounds are formed when two or more pictographs or ideographs are combined to create a completely new character.

e.g.

木 +	木 →	林		means 'a place
mù	mù	lín		overgrown with trees'
wood	wood	forest		(represented by the
				component for 'wood')

手 +	分 +	手 →	掰		means 'to separate
shǒu	fén	shǒu	bāi		something with two
hand	to separate	hand			hands'

Phonetic loan characters make up another group. An example of this is the word lai, which means come. Originally, no character existed for this as it is difficult to depict. The same word can also mean cereal plant 𥝌 𥝌 來

so the character for this was used instead.

Following the introduction of Kaǐ shū, or standard script, between 200 A.D. and 600 A.D., there was no further formal development of the script. However, as new characters can be created using the determinative-phonetic system, the language has continued to grow and evolve.

Structure of Characters

A Chinese character is made up of one or more parts,

e.g.

      one component   日   rì   sun

      two components   女   +   子   →   好   hǎo   good

      three components   亻   +   尔   +   心   →   您   nín   you

The characters are written within the framework of a square, and there are several basic structures.

Basic structure	Form	Examples
Left-right	▌▌	你 nǐ : 亻 尔 你 好 hǎo : 女 子 好 观 guān : 又 见 观 地 dì : 扌 也 地
Top-bottom	▬▬	是 shì : 日 疋 是 要 yào : 西 女 要 星 xīng : 日 生 星
Left-middle-right	▌▌▌	哪 nǎ : 口 月 阝 哪 谢 xiè : 讠 身 寸 谢
Top-middle-bottom	▬▬▬	爱 ài : 爫 冖 友 爱
Symmetrical	◆▮◆	坐 zuò 乘 chéng 爽 shuǎng

The same components may appear in different positions to form different characters:

口 + 马 → 吗 　口 　on the left

囗 + 玉 → 国 　囗 　on the outside

女 + 子 → 好 　子 　on the right

木 + 子 → 李 　子 　at the bottom

日 + 疋 → 是 　日 　at the top

日 + 月 → 明 　日 　on the left

日 + 月 → 明 　月 　on the right

广 + 月 → 有 　月 　at the bottom

Types of Stroke

There are 9 basic strokes:

Stroke	Name of stroke		Writing the stroke	Example Characters	
一	横 héng	(the horizontal)	⟶	不	王
丨	坚 shù	(the vertical)	↓	工	中
丿	撇 piě	(the sweep to the left)	↙	八	人
乀	捺 nà	(the sweep to the right)	↘	大	人
丶	点 diǎn	(the dot)	↘	们	这
ノ	提 tí	(the upward stroke)	↗	汉	我
亅亅乀	钩 gōu	(the hook)	↓⟶↳	字　小	民
フ	横折 héngzhé	(the horizontal turn)	⌐↓	口	日
ㄴ	坚折 shùzhé	(the vertical turn)	ㄴ→	亡	忙

Stroke Sequence

There is a particular sequence in which the strokes must be written. If it is followed, the writing can be smooth and fast.

Stroke Sequence Examples

A horizontal stroke is written before a vertical stroke.	十 shí	一	十		
	干 gān	一	二	干	
The sweeping stroke to the left is written before the sweeping stroke to the right.	八 bā	ノ	八		
	人 rén	ノ	人		
The outside component is written before the inside component.	月 yuè	ノ	刀	月	
	同 tóng	丨	冂	同	
The central component is written first, next the stoke on the left, and then the stroke on the right.	小 xiǎo	亅	小	小	
	水 shuǐ	亅	水	水	
The components inside the unsealed box are written before the last stroke that seals the box.	日 rì	丨	冂	月	日
	国 guó	丨	冂	囯	国
The strokes are written from top to bottom	三 sān	一	二	三	
	京 jīng	亠	古	京	
The strokes are written from left to right.	儿 ér	ノ	儿		
	川 chuān	ノ	川	川	

Continues Strokes

In some characters a couple of the strokes are written continuously,

e.g.   ノ 刀 月 月

Here a horizontal turn and a hook are written as one continuous stroke.
Other strokes may look continous, but are in fact, separate.

女 nǚ

woman;
girl;
daughter

女儿	nǚ ér	daughter
女工	nǚ gōng	woman worker
女皇	nǚ huáng	empress
女人	nǚ rén	woman
女士	nǚ shì	lady
女王	nǚ wáng	queen
女性	nǚ xìng	the female

The original pictograph for woman depicted her in a bowing position 肉.
Apparently, for ease in writing, man reduced this to a humbler form
- a woman kneeling down 叟 - but not for long.
The modern version 女 graphically portrays the big stride woman has
taken to keep up with man.

く	女	女										
1	2	3										

子 zǐ

infant;
child;
son

子弹	zǐ dàn	bullet
子弟	zǐ dì	young generations
子女	zǐ nǚ	children
子孙	zǐ sūn	descendants
子夜	zǐ yè	midnight
子音	zǐ yīn	consonant
孩子	haí zi	child

This character for child originated from a representation of an infant
with outstretched arms and legs. Eventually it was modified to one
with legs swaddled in cloth bands. Evidently, to the Chinese parent,
the secret of infant care lies in keeping one end wet and the other
end dry.

ㄱ	了	子										
1	2	3										

好 hǎo

good;
right;
excellent

好吃	hǎo chī	delicious
好处	hǎo chù	benefit; advantage
好感	hǎo gǎn	good impression
好汉	hǎo hàn	worthy man
好久	hǎo jiǔ	a long time
好看	hǎo kàn	good looking
好听	hǎo tīng	pleasant to the ear

Man combined 女 (girl or daughter) with 子 (child or son) to form a
character for goodness and excellence. From experience he must
have found his greatest good in the possession of a wife and a child
or a son and a daughter. It is also good that his wife sticks to his
child.

く	女	女	女'	奵	好							
1	2	3	4	5	6							

安 ān
peace; contentment

安定	ān dìng	stable
安眠	ān mián	sleep peacefully
安排	ān pái	arrange
安全	ān quán	safe; secure
安慰	ān wèi	comfort; console
安装	ān zhuāng	install; assemble
不安	bù ān	uneasy; worried

The character for peace and contentment is made up of woman (女) and roof (宀). Man conceived the idea that to attain peace he should have only one woman under the roof or confine her within the house.

| 、 | 丷 | 宀 | 它 | 安 | 安 | | | | |
| 1 | 2 | 3 | 4 | 5 | 6 | | | | |

字 zì
written character

字典	zì diǎn	dictionary
字号	zì hào	name of shop
字迹	zì jī	handwriting
字据	zì jù	written receipt
字幕	zì mù	subtitle
字体	zì tǐ	style of calligraphy
写字	xiě zì	writing (words)

To preserve written characters from deterioration man transcribed them on bamboo bound into books. Such precious written words came to be cherished as a child (子) is cherished under a roof (宀). Hence 字 : the written character.
Pictured here under the roof is a precious youthful character being preserved from deterioration.

| 、 | 丷 | 宀 | 宀 | 字 | 字 | | | | |
| 1 | 2 | 3 | 4 | 5 | 6 | | | | |

豕 shǐ
pig

猪排	zhū pái	pork ribs
猪肉	zhū ròu	pork
猪油	zhū yóu	lard
猪肝色	zhū gān sè	maroon colour
懒猪	lǎn zhū	lazy pig

In this pictograph of a pig the head is replaced by a line (一). On the left are the belly and paws (豸) and on the right the back and tail (乀). The domestic pig might well symbolise prosperity to man, so closely knit and tied together were their lives. This interdependence probably gave rise to the proverbial saying: "The schoolmaster should not leave his books, nor the poor man his pig."

| 一 | 丆 | 丁 | 豕 | 豕 | 豕 | 豕 | | | |
| 1 | 2 | 3 | 4 | 5 | 6 | 7 | | | |

家 jiā
house;
family

家产	jiā chǎn	family's property
家具	jiā jù	furniture
家庭	jiā tíng	family; home
家务	jiā wù	household chores
家乡	jiā xiāng	native place
家长	jiā zhǎng	parents
家族	jiā zú	clan or the family

A pig (豕) under the roof (宀) gave man his concept of home (家).
Domesticated, the pig brought man no domestic trouble and was allowed freedom to wander about in the house.

丶 八 宀 宀 宁 宁 穷 家 家 家
1 2 3 4 5 6 7 8 9 10

嫁 jià
to marry
a man

嫁娶	jià qǔ	marriage
嫁人	jià rén	get married
嫁妆	jià zhuāng	trousseau
出嫁	chū jià	be married

This character, derived by adding home (家) to woman (女), provides an incentive for a girl to marry. It applies only to woman who, in marriage, adds to her possessions a husband, a home and a family.

𡿨 女 女 女 女 妤 妤 妤 娇 娇 嫁 嫁 嫁
1 2 3 4 5 6 7 8 9 10 11 12 13

妻 qī
wife

妻舅	qī jiù	brother-in-law
妻室	qī shì	legal wife
妻子	qī zi	wife
贤妻	xián qī	good wife

When man marries woman he puts a broom Ψ into her hand ⇃ bestowing upon her the rulership of the house. Hence 妻: a wife - one who wields the broom, using it to take care of house and home.

一 ㄱ 彐 彐 圭 妻 妻 妻
1 2 3 4 5 6 7 8

木 **mù**
tree; wood

木材	mù cái	timber
术筏	mù fá	wooden raft
木工	mù gōng	carpentry
木瓜	mù guā	papaya
木屐	mù jī	clogs
木匠	mù jiàng	carpenter
木料	mù liào	timber; lumber

This is a pictograph of a tree with its branches (一), trunk (丿) and roots (八). Only the trunk and branches are suggested because 木 also stands for wood. The 木 pictured here didn't stand very long though.

| 一 | 十 | 才 | 木 | | | | | | |
| 1 | 2 | 3 | 4 | | | | | | |

李 **lǐ**
plum or plum tree; also a Chinese surname

李树	lǐ shù	plum tree
李子	lǐ zi	plum
行李	xíng lǐ	baggage; luggage

Owing to its prolific nature and its popularity with children, the plum tree came to be known as the tree (木) the children (子) are fond of. In this idealistic ideograph children were located under the tree, thus: 李 . This, unfortunately, has not always been true in life.

| 一 | 十 | 才 | 木 | 杢 | 李 | 李 | | | |
| 1 | 2 | 3 | 4 | 5 | 6 | 7 | | | |

栖 **qī**
to roost; perch or nest; to live in poverty

栖身	qī shēn	dwell; obtain shelter
栖宿	qī sù	rest for the night
栖息	qī xī	rest

This character is built on tree(木)as radical and wife (妻) as phonetic. The tree provides the base and the wife supplies the sound.
Man simplified it by puting in place of wife, the character for "west" (西).

| 一 | 十 | 才 | 木 | 木' | 木 | 杤 | 栖 | 栖 | 栖 |
| 1 | 2 | 3 | 4 | 5 | 6 | 7 | 8 | 9 | 10 |

人 rén

man;
person;
human

人才	rén cái	men of talent
人格	rén gé	personality
人口	rén kǒu	population
人类	rén lèi	mankind
人民	rén mín	people
人生	rén shēng	the life of man
人为	rén wéi	man-made

The pictographic profile of a person（人）presents an insight into his evolutionary development. Created from earth and equipped with hands and feet, lowly man eked out an existence from the ground with his hands 彡 to help him stand on his feet 冗. Discarding both hands and feet, he used only his head 冗. Today, in the race of the survival of the fittest, he loses his head completely 彳 and finds himself barely able to keep his feet.

ノ	人											
1	2											

大 dà

big; great

大胆	dà dǎn	daring; bold
大概	dà gài	probably
大家	dà jiā	all (people)
大人	dà rén	adult
大声	dà shēng	loud voice
大厦	dà shà	big building
大学	dà xué	university

The ideographic representation for "big" is simply a front elevation of a full-grown man with arms stretched out to the limit 大. What conveys the idea of "big" is not the size of the man but his demonstrative gesture. Some of the assortment of characters pictured below are trying to show what "big" means. Others are merely trying to show off.

一	ナ	大										
1	2	3										

天 tiān

heaven;
sky; day

天才	tiān cái	genius
天空	tiān kōng	sky
天生	tiān shēng	inborn
天下	tiān xià	the whole world
天真	tiān zhēn	naive; innocent
白天	bái tiān	daytime
明天	míng tiān	tomorrow

This stylised representation shows man's ability to stand on his feet（人）, extending his arms egotistically（大）. But high above man（人）, be he ever so great（大）, stretches the heavenly firmament, filling the empty space above his shoulders and directing his footsteps. Hence: 天, meaning heaven - man's rightful and authoritative head. Since the growing light of the sky ushers in the dawn of day, 天 came to mean also "day".

一	二	天	天									
1	2	3	4									

夫 fū

husband; distinguished person

农夫	nóng fū	farmer
懦夫	nuò fū	coward
渔夫	yú fū	fisherman
丈夫	zhàng fū	husband
夫妻	fū qī	husband and wife
夫人	fū rén	wife; madam
大夫	dài fū	medical doctor

A youthful person (人), grown big (大) and attaining maturity at 20, used a hairpin (一) and was vested with the virile cap of manhood 夫 . Given an honourable name, he was considered a distinguished person, qualified as a prospective husband. Hence 夫 means a distinguished person or husband.

一	二	丰	夫			
1	2	3	4			

太 tài

too; over; excessive

太多	tài duō	too many
太后	tài hòu	empress dowager
太监	tài jiàn	eunuch
太空	tài kōng	outer space; sky
太平	tài píng	peace
太太	tài tài	madam
太阳	tài yáng	sun

By underscoring "big" (大) with a line (一) man came up with a superlative character (太) meaning too much or over the limit. In the ecstasy of double happiness and the rapture of material bliss that followed, man bestowed upon his wife a flattering title: 太太 a double emphasis. She lived up to it. Man thereafter reduced the underline to a teeny-weeny stroke 太 .

一	大	大	太			
1	2	3	4			

立 lì

stand; rise up

立场	lì chǎng	standpoint; position
立法	lì fǎ	legislation
立即	lì jí	at once
立刻	lì kè	immediately
立体	lì tǐ	three-dimensional
立足	lì zú	base oneself on
建立	jiàn lì	establish; erect

This character, meaning plain standing or rising up, portrays a person standing - not in the abstract, but on firm, stable ground (一). Originally written 立, it was modified to 立 and finally to 立. Illustrated here are some human characters, firm and infirm, trying to stand on stable ground and demonstrating that plain standing is not plain sailing.

、	二	六	立	立		
1	2	3	4	5		

小 xiǎo

small;
petty;
young

小吃	xiǎo chī	snacks
小丑	xiǎo chǒu	clown
小岛	xiǎo dǎo	small island; islet
小姐	xiǎo jiě	lady; miss
小麦	xiǎo mài	wheat
小时	xiǎo shí	hour
小偷	xiǎo tōu	thief

A vertical stroke, (亅), separating two little ones(八)gave man his concept of "small". The idea was also derived from the division (八) of an object (亅) already small by its nature. To man, division (÷) makes small (小) and multiplication (✕) makes big (大)a thing. Our illustration shows how to multiply happiness by dividing sorrow.

小 small   大 big

| 亅 | 小 | 小 | | | | | | | | | | |
| 1 | 2 | 3 | | | | | | | | | | |

少 shǎo or shào

less; few;
short of

少量	shǎo liàng	small quantity
少女	shào nǚ	young girl
少数	shǎo shù	minority
少许	shǎo xǔ	little; few
少有	shǎo yǒu	rare; scarce
少年	shào nián	teenager
多少	duō shǎo	how many

大 → 小 → 少

This character combines 小 with 丿 to form 少 . It means to cut smaller or diminish (丿) that which is already small (小) , thus making it less (少). To cut short the diminishing process, the method suggested below is an effective short cut to reduce big (大) to small (小) and small (小) to less (少) .

| 亅 | 小 | 小 | 少 | | | | | | | | | |
| 1 | 2 | 3 | 4 | | | | | | | | | |

尖 jiān

pointed;
sharp

尖兵	jiān bīng	vanguard
尖刀	jiān dāo	sharp knife
尖顶	jiān dǐng	peak; apex
尖端	jiān duān	highest point
尖利	jiān lì	sharp
尖锐	jiān ruì	sharp; pointed
尖塔	jiān tǎ	spire

By placing small (小) on top of big (大)man came up with an ideograph to describe anything that tapers from big to small. Hence: 尖 , meaning pointed or sharp or, figuratively, sharp-witted. But not all objects which are small at the top and big at the bottom are sharp or sharp-witted, as the examples on the right prove.

| 亅 | 小 | 小 | 小 | 少 | 尖 | | | | | | | |
| 1 | 2 | 3 | 4 | 5 | 6 | | | | | | | |

田 tián
rice field; grain field

田地	tián dì	field or situation
田鸡	tián jī	frog
田径	tián jìng	track and field
田野	tián yě	open country
田园	tián yuán	fields
耕田	gēng tián	plough

From dawn to dusk man toiled in the field, taking to heart the proverbial saying: "Never leave your field in spring or your house in winter." The character he shaped for "field" was a pictograph of ploughed field with furrows and cross-paths: 田. By the sweat of his brow he reaped the fruits of his labour. But all that toil has left its mark of furrows and cross-paths, not only on the field, but also indelibly on his brow.

丶	冂	日	用	田										
1	2	3	4	5										

力 lì
strength; force; power

力量	lì liàng	physical strength; force
力气	lì qì	effort; strength
力求	lì qiú	strive; make every effort
力争	lì zhēng	endeavour; fight for
人力	rén lì	labour force

The modern version (力) is a powerful graphic impression of the forearm - a symbol of physical strength. Moral strength, however, is more to be desired. And those who go by the rule: "Might is right" will soon have to learn that "Right is might".
In the original form (系) the long middle line (丩), curved at the top to take less room, represents the sinew that binds muscle to bone. The other line (八) pictures the fibrous sheath of the sinew.

フ	力													
1	2													

男 nán
man; male; masculine

男孩	nán hái	boy
男女	nán nǚ	men and women
男人	nán rén	man
男声	nán shēng	male voice
男性	nán xìng	male
男装	nán zhuāng	male attire
男子	nán zi	man; male

A field (田), where strength (力) is exerted, is the symbol for "masculine" man 男, the male of the human species. This is probably because the home is where the female of the same species exerts her strength. Our picture shows strength being exerted - by the male (男) in field-work, the female (女) in housework, and their offspring (子) in promotional work.

丶	冂	日	用	田	罒	男								
1	2	3	4	5	6	7								

日 rì
sun; day

日报	rì bào	daily newspaper
日本	Rì Běn	Japan
日常	rì cháng	daily; usual
日出	rì chū	sunrise
日光	rì guāng	sunshine
日记	rì jì	diary
日历	rì lì	calendar

The sun was first depicted as a circle with an "eye" or centre and rays extending to the corners of the earth. This was simplified to ⊙, then modified: ⊖, and finally squared off: 日. Just as surely as its rising and setting mark the "day" for man, the sun's shining upon the wicked as well as the good demonstrates that it sees the whole world with one eye.

丨	冂	月	日												
1	2	3	4												

月 yuè
moon; month

月饼	yuè bǐng	moon cake
月份	yuè fèn	month
月光	yuè guāng	moonlight
月经	yuè jīng	menstruation
月亮	yuè liàng	moon
月票	yuè piào	monthly ticket
月球	yuè qiú	the moon

To form the character for moon (or lunar month) man chose the crescent. The original pictograph suggested two phases of a waxing new moon. Tilting it: and then directing it earthwards: 月 exposed man to the influence of moonbeam radiation - with striking consequences. Pictured here is a beaming moon casting Its spell on some beaming moon-struck earthlings.

丿	刀	月	月												
1	2	3	4												

明 míng
brilliant; bright; enlightened

明白	míng bái	understand; clear
明亮	míng liàng	shining; bright
明朗	míng lǎng	bright and clear
明年	míng nián	next year
明显	míng xiǎn	obvious
明智	míng zhì	wise

Man combined the sun (日) and the moon (月) to produce an ideograph for bright, brilliant or enlightened. He called it: "ming" (明) and used it also for the brilliant Ming Dynasty of China which came in the wake of the Dark Ages of Europe. Today science and technology has ushered in the dazzling Space Age - with man very much enlightened and the future very much bedarkened.

丨	冂	月	日	旫	明	明	明								
1	2	3	4	5	6	7	8								

白 **bái**
clear; white; plain

白菜	bái cài	Chinese cabbage
白费	bái fèi	in vain; waste
白喉	bái hóu	diphtheria
白色	bái sè	white colour
白糖	bái táng	white sugar
白兔	bái tù	white rabbit
坦白	tǎn bái	frank

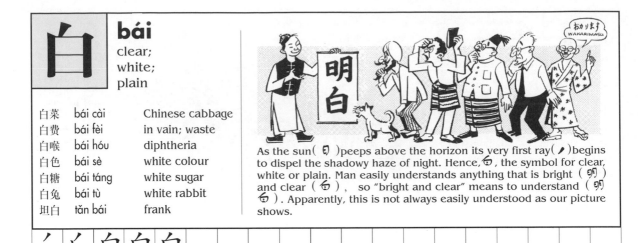

As the sun (日) peeps above the horizon its very first ray (丿) begins to dispel the shadowy haze of night. Hence, 白, the symbol for clear, white or plain. Man easily understands anything that is bright (明) and clear (白), so "bright and clear" means to understand (明白). Apparently, this is not always easily understood as our picture shows.

丿	亻	冂	白	白								
1	2	3	4	5								

旦 **dàn**
dawn; daybreak

旦暮	dàn mù	morning and evening
旦夕	dàn xī	in a short while
花旦	huā dàn	prima dona in an opera
元旦	yuán dàn	New Year's Day
一旦	yī dàn	once; as soon as

The daily appearance of the sun (日) above the horizon (一) gave man his concept of dawn 旦. From the sun's early rising rose the proverbial saying: "To get up early for three mornings is equal to one day of time." Man preached this - from the rising of the sun to its setting - but it never dawned on him to practise it.

丨	冂	冃	日	旦								
1	2	3	4	5								

甲 **jiǎ**
first; armour or protective covering

甲板	jiǎ bǎn	deck of a ship
甲虫	jiǎ chóng	beetle
甲克	jiǎ kè	jacket
甲壳	jiǎ qiào	crust
甲鱼	jiǎ yú	soft-shelled turtle
甲骨文	jiǎ gǔ wén	inscriptions on oracle bones

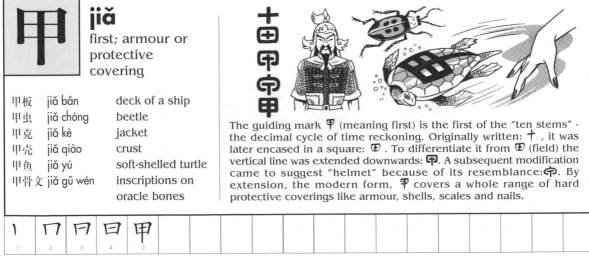

The guiding mark 甲 (meaning first) is the first of the "ten stems" - the decimal cycle of time reckoning. Originally written: 十, it was later encased in a square: 田. To differentiate it from 田 (field) the vertical line was extended downwards: 甲. A subsequent modification came to suggest "helmet" because of its resemblance: 甲. By extension, the modern form, 甲 covers a whole range of hard protective coverings like armour, shells, scales and nails.

丨	冂	冃	日	甲								
1	2	3	4	5								

早 zǎo
early; morning

早安	zǎo ān	good morning
早班	zǎo bān	morning shift
早餐	zǎo cān	breakfast
早操	zǎo cāo	morning exercise
早晨	zǎo chén	early morning
早春	zǎo chūn	early spring
早婚	zǎo hūn	marrying too early

早 (meaning early or morning) is the time of the day when the sun (日) has risen to the height of a man's helmet (十). 十 is the old form of 甲, originally meaning helmet. Since another meaning of 甲 (十) is "first", the character: 早 signifies also the first (十) sun (日), that is, the early morning: 早 .

㇑	口	日	日	旦	早
1	2	3	4	5	6

休 xiū
rest; cease

休会	xiū huì	adjourn (meeting)
休假	xiū jià	on leave
休息	xiū xi	rest or relax
休闲	xiū xián	lie fallow (land)
休想	xiū xiǎng	don't expect
休业	xiū yè	wind up (business)
休战	xiū zhàn	ceasefire

This is a refreshing character for any person (人) working near a shady tree (木). It literally means "rest" (休) and pictures a person (人 or 亻) leaning against a tree (木). Of the tree the Chinese proverb laments: "One generation plants the trees under whose shade another generation takes its ease." Exemplifying this, we show a character leisurely basking in the sunshine and leaning himself against a tree planted by an older generation.

ノ	亻	亻	什	休	休
1	2	3	4	5	6

东 dōng
east

东方	dōng fāng	the East
东风	dōng fēng	east wind
东京	Dōng Jīng	Tokyo
东欧	Dōng Ōu	Eastern Europe
东西	dōng xī	things; East and West

Man turned his head around, looking for a suitable sign for "east" - the direction he faced when he saw the sun rise every day. He succeeded one morning when he observed the sun (日) through the trees (木). So sun (日) behind tree (木) became east (东).Fortunately, success did not turn man's head, otherwise he would have been left facing the wrong direction.

日 + 木 = 東 = 東

一	七	弃	弃	东
1	2	3	4	5

西 xī
west

西边	xī bian	west side
西餐	xī cān	Western-style food
西方	xī fāng	the West
西瓜	xī guā	watermelon
西南	xī nán	southwest
西欧	Xī Ōu	Western Europe
西洋	Xī Yáng	the West

As the sun settles in the west birds roost in their nests; so a cross-hatched bird's nest provided the cradle for "west", and nest became west 鹵. Man's fertile imagination conceived a new ideograph - a nest with a brooding bird: 卤 hatching up a new form: 卤 which finally developed into a full-fledged character for west: 西 . As all "things" exist between east (东) and west (西), the combination east-west, meaning "things", came to be applied to anything from east to west.

一	厂	冂	丙	襾	西					
1	2	3	4	5	6					

上 shàng
up; above; ascend

上班	shàng bān	go to work
上辈	shàng bèi	one's elders
上苍	shàng cāng	Heaven; God
上策	shàng cè	the best plan
上层	shàng céng	upper strata
上等	shàng děng	first-class
上当	shàng dàng	cheated

Since up and down, above and below are relative and abstract terms, man conveyed the ideas graphically by relating a simple stroke to a horizontal foundation line (—). This stroke above the base line was originally a dot: ⟂ extended to a line: 二 propped upright: ⊥. embellished: 止 and finally stabilized: 上 .

一	卜	上								
1	2	3								

下 xià
down; below; descend

下班	xià bān	be off duty
下策	xià cè	bad plan
下层	xià céng	lower level
下场	xià chǎng	end; fate
下沉	xià chén	sink
下等	xià děng	low grade
下级	xià jí	lower level

The concept of down and below is clarified in relation to a horizontal line. The stroke below the fundamental line was originally a dot: 丅 which was extended to a line: 二 for ease in writing. The modified forms: 丅 and 下 eventually led to the final ideograph: 下 . The characters below, although literally under water, are figuratively above water.

一	丁	下								
1	2	3								

中 **zhōng**

centre;
middle;
neutral

中部	zhōng bù	central section
中餐	zhōng cān	Chinese meal
中层	zhōng céng	middle-level
中立	zhōng lì	neutral
中等	zhōng děng	middle-class
中断	zhōng duàn	break off
中间	zhōng jiān	middle

By shooting an arrow: | right into the centre of a square target: 口 man scored a bull's-eye and secured a mark for "centre": 𠙶. He added a decoration of four stripes: 𣥐, rearranged them: 𢀖, stripped them off: 中, and finally hit his mark for simplicity: 中 . The symbol also means standing in the middle or neutrality （中立）. Unfortunately, in the application of neutrality, man has completely missed his mark.

丨 冂 口 中

1 2 3 4

奴 **nú**

slave;
servant

奴婢	nú bì	female slave
奴才	nú cai	flunkey; lackey
奴化	nú huà	enslave
奴隶	nú lì	slave
奴仆	nú pú	male slave
奴性	nú xìng	servile disposition
奴役	nú yì	slavery

A woman 女 under the hand 又 of a master signifies slave. The components 又 and 女 put together literally mean "handmaid" - a female who slaves with her hands. 奴 includes slaves of both sexes who serve their masters hand and foot.

⺄ 𠃌 女 奴 奴

1 2 3 4 5

友 **yǒu**

friend

友爱	yǒu ài	friendly affection
友邦	yǒu bāng	friendly nation
友好	yǒu hǎo	friendly
友情	yǒu qíng	friendship
友人	yǒu rén	friend
友善	yǒu shàn	friendly
友谊	yǒu yì	friendship

The character for "friend" originated with two right hands acting co-operatively in the same direction 𠬞𠬞 and later reaching out to clasp each other in friendship 𠂇又. placing the hands, one upon the other: 𠂇又 and, with a little straightening out, man derived the modern reinforced form: 友 .

一 ナ 方 友

1 2 3 4

手

shǒu
hand

手臂	shǒu bì	arm
手表	shǒu biǎo	wrist-watch
手册	shǒu cè	handbook
手段	shǒu duàn	means; measure
手法	shǒu fǎ	skill; tricks
手工	shǒu gōng	handwork
手铐	shǒu kào	handcuffs

The earliest pictograph for hand placed undue emphasis on the palm lines as basis 𦥑. Practical experience, however, put man on the right lines - the fingers 𦥑. Finally, reinforced with straight lines 𦥑 the character assumed the modern form 手 with fingers of unequal length. For, as the proverb goes, "Of the ten fingers, some are long and some are short." 手 proved handy as radical for numerous characters with its variants 扌 and 𠂤.

一 二 三 手
1 2 3 4

我

wǒ
I; me

我们	wǒ men	we
我爱你	wǒ ài nǐ	I love you
我们的	wǒ men de	our; ours

The earliest forms show two spears against each other in direct confrontation: 𢦏, presumably symbolizing two rights being asserted and, by extension, my right, that is, me. A later transcription projected a new image: 我, a pictograph of a hand 手 grasping a spear 戈, denoting that when man wields in his hand 手 a spear 戈 his ego, the big "I", emerges. Hence 我: I.

一 二 于 手 扰 我 我
1 2 3 4 5 6 7

你

nǐ
you

你好	nǐ hǎo	how do you do
你们	nǐ men	you (plural)
你们的	nǐ men de	your; yours (plural)

The classical character for "you", an equal, was 爾, a pictograph of a balance 爻 loaded with 爻爻 equally on both sides and topped by a phonetic 尒. 爾 was eventually contracted to 尓. By adding 人 (person) to 尓, man introduced the human element and came up with 你 - a person who carries the same weight: you.

丿 亻 亻 你 你 你 你
1 2 3 4 5 6 7

也 yě
also;
in addition
to

也罢	yě bà	let it be
也好	yě hǎo	may as well
也行	yě xíng	all right
也许	yě xǔ	perhaps
也有	yě yǒu	also have

Original the character 也 was a representation of an ancient drinking horn, shaped like a funnel. In addition to his rightful helongings, man also appropriated this drinking vessel. To this day It has remained in his possession - a pictograph specially horrowed for the conjunction "also", joining man to his drinking horn.

丁 力 也
1 2 3

他 tā
he; she

他处	tā chu	elsewhere
他的	tā de	his
他们	tā men	they
他人	tā rén	the other person
他日	tā rì	some other day
他乡	tā xiāng	place far away from home

The character 他 is drawn from 人 (person) and 也 (also). By extension it means "that person also" and refers to the other person: he or she.

丿 亻 彳 什 他
1 2 3 4 5

目 mù
eye

目标	mù biāo	aim
目的	mù dì	purpose; aim; goal
目光	mù guāng	sight; vision; view
目见	mù jiàn	see for oneself
目力	mù lì	eyesight
目前	mù qián	at present
目送	mù sòng	watch somebody go

In its primitive form the eye was pictured naturally with eyelids and pupil. When stylized: Its similarity to (four) deceived man's eye; so It was stood on end: and finally squared off: It would seem that even with hls very own eyes man could not see eye to eye.

丨 冂 月 月 目
1 2 3 4 5

见 jiàn

see

见鬼	jiàn guǐ	preposterous
见解	jiàn jiě	opinions
见面	jiàn miàn	meet
见闻	jiàn wén	knowledge
见习	jiàn xí	learn on the job
见效	jiàn xiào	effective
见笑	jiàn xiào	laugh at (me or us)

For the verb "to see" the eye was set atop man . As the eye grew, man shrank to produce the regular form , now simplified to 见 .

Stroke order: 见 (1 2 3 4)

口 kǒu

mouth; opening

口才	kǒu cái	eloquence
口吃	kǒu chī	stutter
口臭	kǒu chòu	bad breath
口袋	kǒu dài	pocket
口福	kǒu fú	gourmet's luck
口供	kǒu gòng	testimony
口号	kǒu hào	slogan

The character for mouth was originally a pictograph of an open mouth: broadening into a smile: and eventually stiffening: and contracting to a square: . also means an opening. But beware: "Mischief comes from much opening of the mouth".

Stroke order: 口 (1 2 3)

言 yán

words; speak

言辞	yán cí	one's words
言和	yán hé	make peace
言论	yán lùn	speech
言谈	yán tán	the way one speaks
言行	yán xíng	words and deeds
言语	yán yǔ	spoken language

"In a multitude of words," the Chinese saying goes, "there will certainly be a mistake." This is evident from the character for words itself: 言. Originally written , it represented a mouth from which issued a mistake (an old form of). Apparently, to correct this error, man changed to .So today, with great care, his mouth speaks its lines , transforming soundwaves into words: 言 .

Stroke order: 言 (1 2 3 4 5 6 7)

工 **gōng**

work;
labour;
skill

工厂	gōng chǎng	factory
工党	Gōng Dǎng	the Labour Party
工地	gōng dì	construction site
工夫	gōng fu	time; effort
工具	gōng jù	tools
工会	gōng huì	trade union
工匠	gōng jiàng	craftsman

工 is a pictograph of the ancient workman's square or carpenter's ruler. By extension, it means work, labour or skill. An early form: 工 included three parallel lines traced with the square. Man has always had problems with work and remuneration. Instead of striving for prosperity through work, he works for prosperity through strife, as our picture of master and servant shows.

一	丁	工							
1	2	3							

左 **zuǒ**

left;
also a Chinese
surname

左边	zuǒ bian	left side
左面	zuǒ miàn	left side
左派	zuǒ pài	leftist
左倾	zuǒ qīng	left-leaning
左手	zuǒ shǒu	left hand
左翼	zuǒ yì	left wing
左右	zuǒ yòu	left and right

The character for left: 左 depicts the hand 𠂇 that holds the carpenter's square 工 - the left. The left hand 𠂇 is meant to help its more skilled correlative member in manual work 工 as, for example, holding the ruler while the right hand draws the line. 左 stands for the direction left.

一	𠂇	左	左	左					
1	2	3	4	5					

右 **yòu**

right

右边	yòu bian	right side
右面	yòu miàn	right side
右派	yòu pài	rightist
右倾	yòu qīng	right deviation
右手	yòu shǒu	right hand
右翼	yòu yì	right wing
向右	xiàng yòu	turn right

The character for right: 右 is simply a hand 𠂇 and a mouth 口, signifying the hand you eat with the right. 右 stands for the direction right.

一	𠂇	才	右	右					
1	2	3	4	5					

舌

shé
tongue

舌尖	shé jiān	tip of the tongue
舌头	shé tou	tongue
舌音	shé yīn	lingual sounds
舌战	shé zhàn	heated discussion

"The tongue is like a sharp knife; It kills without drawing blood," so warns the Chinese proverb. Exemplifying this, early forms of the character show a forked tongue thrust viciously out of the mouth: ₅. It skilfully smoothens itself: ₃ and finally straightens: ₃ into the new form: 舌.

ノ	二	千	千	舌	舌					
1	2	3	4	5	6					

话

huà
talk;
speech;
language

话别	huà bié	say goodbye
话柄	huà bǐng	subject for ridicule
话旧	huà jiù	talk about old time
话剧	huà jù	stage play
话题	huà tí	subject of a talk
笑话	xiào huà	joke

Man combined words 言 and tongue 舌 to produce 话, meaning speech or language. To emphasize the importance of weighing words before delivery and to caution against their indiscriminating proliferation, the Chinese proverb warns: "water and words are easy to pour out but impossible to recover."

`	讠	讠	讠	话	话	话	话			
1	2	3	4	5	6	7	8			

耳

ěr
ear

耳朵	ěr duo	ear
耳光	ěr guāng	a box on the ear
耳环	ěr huán	earrings
耳机	ěr jī	earphones
耳孔	ěr kǒng	earhole
耳鸣	ěr míng	tinnitus
耳目	ěr mù	informer

From time immemorial man discerned the wisdom of listening. He proclaimed from ear to ear the proverbial saying: "A good talker is inferior to a good listener." The pictograph created for the listening ear began with a natural rendition: ⬓ and ended with a stylised form: 耳. His talking about the listening ear began also with a natural rendition, but It doesn't seem like ever ending in any form.

一	丆	丌	刅	耵	耳					
1	2	3	4	5	6					

取 qǔ

take;
select;
seize

取代	qǔ dài	replace
取道	qǔ dào	by way of; via
取得	qǔ dé	obtain
取缔	qǔ dì	ban; suppress
取决	qǔ jué	be decided by
取巧	qǔ qiǎo	resort to trickery
取消	qǔ xiāo	cancel

To secure a firm hold on a person the hand 又 is laid on the ear 耳. A hand on the ear, then, means to take hold of, to neglect or seize: 取 Pictured here are various characters extending a helping hand to demonstrate what 取 means.

一	厂	厂	F	F	耳	耳	耶	取												
1	2	3	4	5	6	7	8													

兄 xiōng

elder
brother

兄弟	xiōng dì	brothers
兄长	xiōng zhǎng	respectful form of address for an elder brother or a man friend
长兄	zhǎng xiōng	elder brother

The concept of "older brother" is suggested by the ideograph 兄 which combines person 人 with mouth 口. Ideally, 兄 represents a person 人 characterized by a large mouth 口, i.e., one who speaks with authority to exhort or correct a younger brother. Our picture shows what could happen in reality if big mouth of "older brother" went into action.

丶	口	口	尸	兄																
1	2	3	4	5																

八 bā

eight

八仙	Bā Xiān	The Eight Immortals
八月	bā yuè	August
八字	bā zì	Eight Characters (indicating the time of a person's birth, used in fortune telling).

In the etymological sense, 八 means to divide or separate. It is made up of two separate strokes, forming a symmetrical symbol 八. Probably because the number 8 can be easily divided and subdivided, 八 (to divide) came to stand for 8, the much-divisible number. The original seal form: 八, coincidentally, has 8 lines.

丿	八																			
1	2																			

兑 duì
exchange; barter

兑付	duì fù	cash (a cheque, etc)
兑换	duì huàn	exchange
兑现	duì xiàn	pay cash
兑换表	duì huàn biǎo	exchange table

The character 兑 originally meant to speak, bless or rejoice. It was derived from older brother's 兄 dissipation of effluent breath 八 into words of encouragement: 兑 involving the exchange of words. With money talking louder than words in man's affluent society, there arose the need to exchange the old meaning, for a new one. Today, 兑 means to exchange money or to barter.

1	2	3	4	5	6	7
丶	丷	丷	出	台	尸	兑

十 shí
ten

十分	shí fēn	very; fully
十万	shí wàn	one hundred thousand
十月	shí yuè	October
十足	shí zú	100 per cent
十二月	shí èr yuè	December
十一月	shí yī yuè	November
十字架	shí zì jià	cross

十 is a symbol of completeness. It represents extent in two dimensions 十 (一 and 丨) and is formed by joining the five cardinal points: east, west, south, north and centre: 十. The sign is therefore an appropriate symbol for the numeral 10 - a complete number containing all the other simple numbers of decimal numeration. Our picture illustrates the completeness of 10, both in number and extent.

1	2
一	十

古 gǔ
old; ancient; also a Chinese surname

古巴	Gǔ Bā	Cuba
古代	gǔ dài	ancient times
古典	gǔ diǎn	classical
古董	gǔ dǒng	antique
古怪	gǔ guài	peculiar; strange
古国	gǔ guó	ancient state
古旧	gǔ jiù	archaic

This character 古 is applicable to that which has passed through ten 十 mouths 口 -a tradition dating back ten generations. It includes anything very old, ancient, of antiquity - whether valuable, invaluable or valueless. Our picture illustrates the process of passing through ten mouths something of questionable value.

1	2	3	4	5
一	十	古	古	古

心 xīn
heart

心爱	xīn ài	dear
心得	xīn dé	personal insight
心烦	xīn fán	vexed
心理	xīn lǐ	psychology
心目	xīn mù	frame of mind
心情	xīn qíng	state of mind
心思	xīn si	thought; idea

The original pictograph was a representation of the physical heart. Its membranous sac was ripped open, exposing it: ⱴ and a delineation of the aorta appended below: ⱴ. A stylization: ⱴ provided the basis for the modern form: 心. Recognition of this vital organ's role as seat of motivation for both good and evil prompted man to take to heart the ancient saying: "Honey mouth, dagger heart."

怒 nù
anger; rage; passion

怒斥	nù chì	rebuke angrily
怒吼	nù hǒu	howl
怒火	nù huǒ	fury
怒气	nù qì	rage; fury
怒容	nù róng	angry look
怒色	nù sè	angry look
愤怒	fèn nù	angry

The very sinister structure of 怒, meaning anger or passion, constitutes a warning to man, for 怒 was secured by bonding slave 奴 to heart 心. It cautions against giving way to anger or passion and becoming slave and handmaid 奴 to the dictates of the heart 心.

怕 pà
fear

怕人	pà rén	terrifying
怕生	pà shēng	shy with strangers
怕死	pà sǐ	fear death
怕羞	pà xiū	bashful; shy
害怕	hài pà	scared
怕事	pà shì	afraid of getting into trouble

The character for fear has, for radical, 忄 - a variant of heart 心. The phonetic, sound component 白 (white) collaborates with the radical, 心 (heart) to instil the idea of fear into this character: 怕, which literally means: "white heart", i.e., fear or lack of courage. Sometimes a "white heart" can inspire the bold deeds of a "lion-heart" as our picture shows.

身 shēn
body

身材	shēn cái	figure (body)
身份	shēn fèn	social status
身价	shēn jià	social status
身躯	shēn qū	body; stature
身世	shēn shì	one's lot
身体	shēn tǐ	body
身心	shēn xīn	body and mind

This character originally meant "pregnant"; it pictured a human figure with prominent belly and one leg thrust forward to support and balance the body: 身. The modern form: 身 also means "the human body" - either' male or female, ordinary or outstanding. We show a couple of outstanding ones - outstanding in "body", not in form or figure.

ノ	イ	门	白	白	身	身							
1	2	3	4	5	6	7							

自 zì
self; oneself

自白	zì bái	self-confession
自动	zì dòng	automatic
自杀	zì shā	commit suicide
自首	zì shǒu	give oneself up
自传	zì zhuàn	autobiography
自己	zì jǐ	oneself
自立	zì lì	independent

Because the nose sticks out most from the face - sometimes too far out - it characterizes the person and symbolizes his personality. A pictographic representation of the nose therefore personifies, not the nose, but "self" or "oneself". Our picture emphasizes the dominant role of the nose in a confrontation of personalities.

ノ	イ	门	自	自	自								
1	2	3	4	5	6								

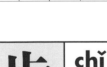

齿 chǐ
teeth

齿轮	chǐ lún	gear-wheel
齿腔	chǐ qiāng	dental cavity
齿痛	chǐ tòng	toothache
齿龈	chǐ yín	the gums
牙·齿	yá chǐ	tooth

The evolutionary struggle of this character sees man fighting a losing battle. Earliest forms show the mouth filled with teeth: 齒 and later only the front teeth: 齒. The regular form: 齒 has the teeth sharpened and capped by the phonetic: 止. The simplified version: 齿 drastically reduces the remaining teeth to one. But, with all that loss, man can still console himself that many a true word is spoken through false teeth.

丨	卜	止	止	齿	齿	齿	齿						
1	2	3	4	5	6	7	8						

止 zhǐ

halt;
stop

止步	zhǐ bù	halt; stop
止境	zhǐ jìng	limit; end
止渴	zhǐ kě	quench thirst
止咳	zhǐ ké	relieve a cough
止痛	zhǐ tòng	allay pains
止血	zhǐ xuè	stop bleeding
停止	tíng zhǐ	halt; stop

Although this character is a crude representation of the motionless foot, with the five toes reduced to three, it does not stand for "foot". Its meanings are derived by extension and include: to halt, stop or stand still. Our illustration shows how, in an emergency, the foot can come in handy to express the idea of "Stop!"

丨 卜 止 止

正 zhèng

straight;
upright;
correct; exact

正当	zhèng dàng	proper; rightful
正派	zhèng pài	upright; decent
正确	zhèng què	correct; right
正式	zhèng shì	official
正统	zhèng tǒng	orthodox
正义	zhèng yì	justice
正月	zhèng yuè	January

The character: 正 shows a foot: 止 (meaning "stop") with a straight line above it. It signifies arrival and stopping (止) at the line or proper limit (一) without going astray. It is also an ideograph of a foot walking in a straight line: 正. Hence the extended meanings: straight, upright, proper, correct, exact.

一 丁 下 正 正

是 shì

right; yes;
am; are; is

是的	shì de	yes; right
是非	shì fēi	right and wrong
是否	shì fǒu	whether or not?
是故	shì gù	for this reason
不是	bù shì	not so

This ideograph locates the sun: 日 over the character for right or correct: 正 (modified to 疋). It depicts the sun: 日 exactly on the meridian: 是. The sun is here taken as the standard for correctness. Hence the idea of "right; yes; am, are, is."

丶 冂 日 日 旦 早 早 昇 是

走 zǒu
walk; run; hasten; depart

走动	zǒu dòng	move around
走狗	zǒu gǒu	running dog; lackey
走廊	zǒu láng	corridor
走路	zǒu lù	walk
走私	zǒu sī	smuggling
走失	zǒu shī	be lost

In the original seal form: 盉 the upper part: 夭 (or 土) represents a man: 大 bending his head: ノ forward to walk rapidly. The lower part: 㐅 (or 止) means "to stop." This combination of bending and stopping indicates walking. The movement is also suggested by the bending: 夭 (土) of the toes or foot: in swift walking. Pictured here are a host of characters. 㐅 (止) walking, running, fleeing - all bending forward but not stopping.

一	十	土	キ	キ	走	走								
1	2	3	4	5	6	7								

土 tǔ
earth; soil; ground

土地	tǔ dì	land
土匪	tǔ fěi	bandit
土话	tǔ huà	local dialect
土壤	tǔ rǎng	soil
土人	tǔ rén	native
土质	tǔ zhì	property of soil
泥土	ní tǔ	soil, earth

Man has always been dependent on the ground for subsistence. To him, earth (土) is represented by its two layers (二) - the topsoil and subsoil - from which growing plants sprout (丨). Hence 土: the good earth that produces all things for man. Pictured here are some such "earthy" provisions.

一	十	土												
1	2	3												

坐 zuò
to sit; a seat

坐牢	zuò láo	be imprisoned
坐落	zuò luò	locate; situate
坐视	zuò shì	sit by and watch
坐位	zuò wèi	seat
坐下	zuò xià	sit down
请坐	qǐng zuò	please sit down

坐, the ideograph for "sit", depicts two men talking face-to-face (从), sitting on the ground (土) but not quite down-to-earth. Although the radical 土 (earth) provides the base for the men (从) to "sit" 坐 on, it can prove to be the root of unproductive activity, as illustrated.

ノ	人	人ノ	从	丛	坐	坐								
1	2	3	4	5	6	7								

出 chū
go out;
issue;
produce

出版	chū bǎn	publish
出产	chū chǎn	produce
出国	chū guó	go abroad
出境	chū jìng	leave a country
出口	chū kǒu	export
出来	chū lai	come out
出卖	chū mài	betray

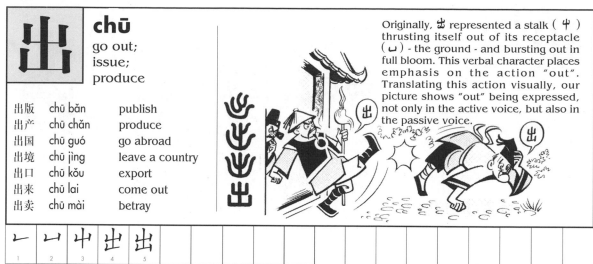

Originally, 出 represented a stalk (屮) thrusting itself out of its receptacle (凵) - the ground - and bursting out in full bloom. This verbal character places emphasis on the action "out". Translating this action visually, our picture shows "out" being expressed, not only in the active voice, but also in the passive voice.

㇄	凵	屮	出	出										
1	2	3	4	5										

生 shēng
produce;
bear;
grow

生病	shēng bìng	fall ill
生存	shēng cún	survive
生动	shēng dòng	vivid
生活	shēng huó	livelihood
生理	shēng lǐ	physiology
生命	shēng mìng	life
生气	shēng qì	angry

The earth (土), producing a plant (屮), lays the groundwork for growth (生). Hence the modified form: 生 , meaning to produce, bear or grow. Man, born imperfect, grows in different ways and directions. Pictured here are examples from three generations.

ノ	㇒	亠	牛	生										
1	2	3	4	5										

姓 xìng
surname

姓名	xìng míng	surname and name
姓谱	xìng pǔ	genealogical record; family register
姓氏	xìng shì	surname
百姓	bǎi xìng	common people
贵姓	guì xìng	what is your surname?

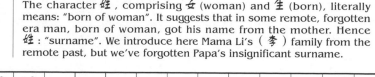

The character 姓 , comprising 女 (woman) and 生 (born), literally means: "born of woman". It suggests that in some remote, forgotten era man, born of woman, got his name from the mother. Hence 姓 : "surname". We introduce here Mama Li's (李) family from the remote past, but we've forgotten Papa's insignificant surname.

㇄	女	女	女	妇	妡	姓	姓							
1	2	3	4	5	6	7	8							

贝 bèi
shells;
valuables

贝雕	bèi diāo	shell carving
贝壳	bèi ké	shell
贝类	bèi lèi	shellfish
贝玉	bèi yù	valuables; gems
贝子	bèi zi	cowries-used as currency in ancient times

This character is a pictograph of the precious cowrie shell. Used in early feudal times as money, it came to mean also "valuables". The regular form（貝）shows a live shell with feelers; but today, like the money it once represented, the shell reveals its hollowness in the simplified form（贝）.

丨 冂 贝 贝
1 2 3 4

贱 jiàn
strength;
force;
power

贱价	jiàn jià	cheap; low-priced
贱卖	jiàn mài	cheap-sale
贫贱	pín jiàn	poor and humble

Two spears: 戔 shattering and destroying the value of shells: 贝, once used as money, conveys the idea of cheap, worthless, mean or humble. Man applied this word to anything of little value, uttering the proverbial saying: "Cheap things are of little value; valuable things are not cheap". In mock humility, he appl!ed it also to himself.

丨 冂 贝 贝 贝一 贝二 贱 贱 贱
1 2 3 4 5 6 7 8 9

贵 guì
expensive;
dear;
honourable

贵宾	guì bīn	guest of honour
贵妇	guì fù	noblewoman
贵姓	guì xìng	your name, please
贵重	guì zhòng	valuable; precious
贵族	guì zú	aristocrat; noble
宝贵	bǎo guì	precious

A basket or container: 虫 (or 虫) filled with precious cowries: 贝 (once used as money) means dear or expensive. By extension, it also means high-class or honourable. In this connection, humble self（贱）thanks honourable readers（贵）for their appreciation and interest in the Bilingual Page.

丶 冖 口 中 虫 串 贵 贵 贵
1 2 3 4 5 6 7 8 9

水

shuǐ
water

水彩	shuǐ cǎi	water colour
水池	shuǐ chí	pond; pool
水沟	shuǐ gōu	drain; ditch
水管	shuǐ guǎn	water pipe
水果	shuǐ guǒ	fruit
水库	shuǐ kù	reservoir; dam
水泥	shuǐ ní	cement

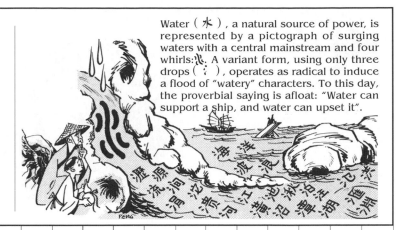

Water (水), a natural source of power, is represented by a pictograph of surging waters with a central mainstream and four whirls:. A variant form, using only three drops (氵), operates as radical to induce a flood of "watery" characters. To this day, the proverbial saying is afloat: "Water can support a ship, and water can upset it".

丿 丬 才 水
1 2 3 4

永

yǒng
everlasting;
perpetual;
forever

永生	yǒng shēng	eternal life
永别	yǒng bié	part forever
永不	yǒng bù	never
永固	yǒng gù	permanently fixed
永恒	yǒng héng	eternal; everlasting
永久	yǒng jiǔ	permanent

One generation comes and another goes, but water flows on incessantly in a continuous cycle. From this unceasing flow of water came the ideograph for "everlasting": 永 - a variation of water (水), with foams and ripples added: 永. 永 will long be remembered as the "everlasting" character that embodies the eight fundamental strokes used in calligraphy.

丶 丁 刁 永 永
1 2 3 4 5

冰

bīng
ice

冰雹	bīng báo	hailstones
冰川	bīng chuān	glacier
冰岛	Bīng Dǎo	Iceland
冰冻	bīng dòng	freeze
冰块	bīng kuài	ice-cube
冰冷	bīng lěng	ice-cold
冰凉	bīng liáng	ice-cold

The character for ice was originally: 仌, representing cracks or crystals on the surface of ice. The radical 冫 depicts water dripping and freezing into an icicle. 冫 was added to 水 (water) to freeze and crystallize it into "frozen water" or ice: 冰. Our illustration applies 冰 figuratively, contrasting icy coldness with fiery passion.

丶 冫 刂 刁 冰 冰
1 2 3 4 5 6

雨 **yǔ** rain

雨点	yǔ diǎn	raindrop
雨季	yǔ jì	rainy season
雨量	yǔ liàng	rainfall
雨伞	yǔ sǎn	umbrella
雨水	yǔ shuǐ	rain water
雨天	yǔ tiān	rainy day
雨衣	yǔ yī	raincoat

雨, the character for rain, is a picture of raindrops (＝＝) falling vertically down (|) from a cloud (冂) in the heavens (一). Not all welcome the rain as showers of blessing from heaven for, as the saying goes, "The farmer hopes for rain, the traveller for fine weather."

一 厂 冂 币 雨 雨 雨 雨
1 2 3 4 5 6 7 8

云 **yún** cloud

云彩	yún cǎi	cloud
云层	yún céng	layers of cloud
云雾	yún wù	mist; fog
云霞	yún xiá	rosy clouds
云霄	yún xiāo	the skies
云烟	yún yān	cloud and mist
白云	bái yún	white clouds

When the humid and warm vapours (ß or ㄥ) rise (㇗ or) and reach the colder regions, they condense and form clouds: 云. Loading the clouds (云) with rain (雨) produces the regular form: 雲. The simplified version relieves the clouds (雲) of their load, reverting the character to its original form: 云.

一 二 云 云
1 2 3 4

雪 **xuě** snow

雪白	xuě bái	snow-white
雪崩	xuě bēng	snowslide
雪恨	xuě hèn	avenge
雪花	xuě huā	snowflake
雪茄	xuě jiā	cigar
雪景	xuě jǐng	snow scenery
雪亮	xuě liàng	bright as snow

The seal character 霅 associates rain 雨 with broom 彗. The modern character 雪 relates rain 雨 to hand ヨ (a contraction of 彗, broom). Both versions fittingly symbolize snow, i.e., rain 雨 which can be taken up in the hand (ヨ) or swept away by a broom (彗).

一 厂 户 币 币 雫 雪 雪 雪 雪 雪
1 2 3 4 5 6 7 8 9 10 11

电 diàn
lightning; electricity

电报	diàn bào	telegram; cable
电池	diàn chí	battery
电工	diàn gōng	electrician
电话	diàn huà	telephone
电流	diàn liú	electric current
电脑	diàn nǎo	computer
电视	diàn shì	television

A streak of lightning (电) amidst the falling rain (雨) forged the character for lightning: 電. Lightning being a visible discharge of electricity, 電 came to mean also electricity. 電 takes the path of least resistance, discharging eight of its thirteen strokes to transform itself into the simplified form: 电.

丶	冂	冃	日	电												
1	2	3	4	5												

雷 léi
thunder

雷达	léi dá	radar
雷鸣	léi míng	thunderous
雷声	léi shēng	thunderclap
雷雨	léi yǔ	thunderstorm
打雷	dǎ léi	to thunder
地雷	dì léi	land-mine
水雷	shuǐ léi	sea-mine

From experience, man knows that rain clouds (雨) over his fields (田) means thunder: 雷, the voice of lightning. The original version of 雷 has three or four fields (畾) incorporated in a graphic pattern to express the reverberation of thunder. To man, thunder is impressive, but it is lightning that does the work.

丶	一	广	冚	乊	乯	乯	雫	雯	雯	雸	雷	雷				
1	2	3	4	5	6	7	8	9	10	11	12	13				

伞 sǎn
umbrella

伞兵	sǎn bīng	paratroop; parachuter
雨伞	yǔ sǎn	umbrella
降落伞	jiàng luò sǎn	parachute

伞 is a pictograph of an umbrella. Its radical: 人 (man) has nothing to do with the original character: 傘. Nevertheless, the regular form: 傘 seems to be harbouring four persons (众) not included in the simplified version: 伞. Under cover of the umbrella, man counsels for the rainy day: "When the sky is clear, carry an umbrella; though your stomach is full, carry provisions."

丿	人	仌	仝	仐	伞											
1	2	3	4	5	6											

川 chuān
river; stream

| 川资 | chuān zī | travelling expenses |
| 四川 | Sì Chuān | Sichuan, China |

"The great river does not reject little stream." As the river meanders through arid land, infusing life into the fields, it is continually fed by little streams. Fittingly, the river is portrayed as flowing water formed by the union of little streams, upon which it vitally depends: 川.The modern independent form: 川 uses a variant: 巛 to serve as source for other related characters.

| 丿 | 川 | 川 |
| 1 | 2 | 3 |

山 shān
mountain; hill

山顶	shān dǐng	mountain top
山歌	shān gē	folk song
山谷	shān gǔ	valley
山脉	shān mài	mountain range
山坡	shān pō	hill slope
山头	shān tóu	hilltop
山崖	shān yá	cliff

A mountain range, with three towering peaks, provides the structure for this pictograph of mountain or hill: 山. From a high vantage point, man is able to oversee what is easily overlooked on a lower plane. Hence the proverb: "If you don't climb the high mountain, you can't view the plain."

| 丨 | 山 | 山 |
| 1 | 2 | 3 |

鸟 niǎo
bird

鸟巢	niǎo cháo	bird's nest
鸟瞰	niǎo kàn	bird's eye view
鸟类	niǎo lèi	birds
鸟笼	niǎo lóng	bird cage
鸟爪	niǎo zhǎo	bird's claws
鸟兽	niǎo shòu	birds and animals
小鸟	xiǎo niǎo	small bird

The regular form: 鳥 is a representation of a long-tailed bird, flaunting its beauty and revelling in its freedom. Unfortunately, beauty has not always been an asset to the bird for, as the saying goes, "It's the beautiful bird that we put in the cage." Tragically, the simplified form sees the poor bird stripped of its plumage: 鸟.

| 丿 | 勹 | 勺 | 鸟 | 鸟 |
| 1 | 2 | 3 | 4 | 5 |

岛 dǎo
island

岛国	dǎo guó	island state
岛屿	dǎo yǔ	islands
半岛	bàn dǎo	peninsula
群岛	qún dǎo	archipelago

Sea-birds often nest on mountainous rocks that emerge from the sea. Hence a bird (鳥) over a mountain (山) gave the concept for island: 島. The ancient form shows a bird hovering over a mountain, with feet visible: 嶌. The modern version has the bird settling on it, with feet hidden: 島, probably hatching the simplified character: 岛.

′	⺈	⺈	鸟	鸟	岛	岛						
1	2	3	4	5	6	7						

飞 fēi
fly

飞机师	fēi jī shī	pilot
飞禽走兽	fēi qín zǒu shòu	birds and beasts

This character draws its inspiration from the migratory flight of the crane - with the long neck of the bird folded on itself: 乑. The flight is speeded up by simplifying the regular form: 飛, lightening its load of strokes from nine to three: 飞.

乁	飞	飞										
1	2	3										

羽 yǔ
feathers; wings

羽毛	yǔ máo	feather
羽毛球	yǔ máo qiú	badminton

Feathers - the showy plumage of birds - are represented by a pair of wings. Like human nature, feathers have changed little in character through the ages. From the original 羿 to 羿 and finally 羽, all look alike at a glance. To confirm this, our illustration takes a closer look at some birds of a feather.

⺆	⺔	习	羽	羽	羽							
1	2	3	4	5	6							

习 xí
practise

习惯	xí guàn	habit
习气	xí qì	bad habit
习俗	xí sú	custom; tradition
习题	xí tí	exercise (of school work)
习性	xí xìng	habits and characteristics

This ideograph combines wings (羽) with self (白, contraction of 自), suggesting a young bird learning to fly by itself; by extension, to practise: 習. Copying the bird, man also tries to fly by speeding up the simplification of the original intricate character: 習, using only one wing for "practice": 习. Woe betide the bird that copies man!

丁	刁	习							
1	2	3							

扇 shàn
fan

扇动	shān dòng	fan; flap
扇惑	shān huò	incite; agitate
扇形	shàn xíng	fan-shaped
扇子	shàn zi	fan
一扇门	yí shàn mén	a door

In this ideograph, a wing (羽) is likened to the leaf of a door (户) in that its attachment is at the end, and both are capable of vibrating and spreading out like a fan: 扇. The combination of these two related components enforces the idea of "fan" (扇), a useful and decorative device often made of feathers (羽).

、	丶	㇆	户	戶	戶	肩	扇	扇	扇
1	2	3	4	5	6	7	8	9	10

鱼 yú
fish

鱼饵	yú ěr	fish-bait
鱼钩	yú gōu	fish-hook
鱼雷	yú léi	torpedo
鱼鳞	yú lín	fish-scales
鱼群	yú qún	shoal of fish
鱼网	yú wǎng	fishing net
鱼肝油	yú gān yóu	cod-liver oil

鱼 is a pictograph of the fish, whose predatory habits prompt man to snap at his own fishy way of life: "Big fish eat small fish; small fish eat water insects; water insects eat weeds and mud." The tail of the fish: proves to be its fiery end, being a form of fire (火), presumably kindled as man prepares to eat big fish.

⺈	⺈	⺈	刍	刍	鱼	鱼	鱼		
1	2	3	4	5	6	7	8		

渔 yú
fishing

渔村	yú cūn	fishing-village
渔夫	yú fū	fisherman
渔港	yú gǎng	fishing port
渔歌	yú gē	fisherman's song
渔民	yú mín	fisherman
渔业	yú yè	fishery
渔舟	yú zhōu	fishing boat

Fish (鱼) and water (氵) are requisites for fishing (渔). The ancient form for fishing reveals water teeming with fishes: 爩. The modified form sees the number reduced to one, probably due to success in fishing: 爩. Disclosed here is yet another form of fishing - without fish or water - but it doesn't look too successful.

`	˙	氵	氵	氵	泸	泸	渔	渔	渔	渔
1	2	3	4	5	6	7	8	9	10	11

鲁 lǔ
stupid; simple

| 鲁钝 | lǔ dùn | stupid |
| 鲁莽 | lǔ mǎng | reckless; careless |

In his eagerness to acquire an ideograph for simple or stupid, man literally acted the part. He appended to fish (鱼) a representation of a nose (旬) which was later corrupted to 曰 (speak). The tragic result: a "dumb" fish unable to speak and a "nosey" one, without scent or sense: 鲁. Simple man, like stupid fish, sees the bait, not the hook.

⺍	⺆	⺈	鱼	鱼	角	鱼	鱼	鲁	鲁	鲁	鲁
1	2	3	4	5	6	7	8	9	10	11	12

羊 yáng
sheep; goat

羊角	yáng jiǎo	ram's horn
羊毛	yáng máo	sheep's wool
羊排	yáng pái	mutton chop
羊皮	yáng pí	sheep skin
羊群	yáng qún	flock of sheep
羊肉	yáng ròu	mutton

Because of its mild and gentle nature, the sheep (羊) is a fitting symbol for meekness. Its pictographic representations take on well-balanced forms. Early versions show frontal views of the head; later modifications fill in the horns, ears, legs and tail. When combined with other components, the tail is often left out: 羊 .

`	⺍	兰	兰	兰	羊
1	2	3	4	5	6

鲜 xiān
fresh

鲜果	xiān guǒ	fresh fruit
鲜红	xiān hóng	bright red
鲜花	xiān huā	fresh flower
鲜美	xiān měi	delicious; tasty
鲜明	xiān míng	vividness
鲜奶	xiān nǎi	fresh milk
鲜血	xiān xuè	blood

This character combines two types of flesh: fish（鱼）and sheep（羊）. Although meat was usually preserved by salting, drying or smoking, ancient man preferred to eat the flesh of fish and sheep fresh. Hence, fish（鱼）and sheep（羊）put together means "fresh": 鲜. In other words, "flesh" becomes "fresh".

ノ	ク	ク	乌	甸	角	鱼	鱼	鱼	鱼'	鲈	鲜	鲜	鲜		
1	2	3	4	5	6	7	8	9	10	11	12	13	14		

美 měi
strength;
force;
power

美观	měi guān	nice looking
美好	měi hǎo	fine; glorious
美化	měi huà	beautiful
美景	měi jǐng	beautiful scenery
美丽	měi lì	beautiful
美梦	měi mèng	fond dream
美妙	měi miào	splendid

This beautifully proportioned character is shaped from 羊 (sheep) and 大 (big). 大 originally represented a person grown big; 羊 is an animal admired for its peace-loving virtue. Ideographically, a mature person（大）who has the mild and gentle disposition of a sheep（羊）regarded as beautiful, admirable: 美.

`	ヾ	ソ	⸲	半	羊	羊	美	美					
1	2	3	4	5	6	7	8	9					

义 yì
justice;
righteousness

义愤	yì fèn	indignation
义务	yì wù	obligation; duty
义演	yì yǎn	benefit performance
意义	yì yì	meaning
正义	zhèng yì	justice

When justice（義）prevails, the aggressive "I": 我 (with spear 戈 in hand 手) becomes subdued like a docile and gentle sheep（羊）. Hence 義 justifies itself as a symbol for right conduct. For the sake of righteousness the regular form is now slashed to three strokes, transforming it into a simplified and perfectly balanced justice: 义.

ノ	义	义					
1	2	3					

yáng
ocean;
foreign

洋葱	yáng cōng	onion
洋行	yáng háng	foreign firm
洋化	yáng huà	westernized
洋灰	yáng huī	cement
洋人	yáng rén	foreigner
洋溢	yáng yì	fill with
海洋	hǎi yáng	ocean

Although 羊 is a phonetic, it also serves to emphasize the meaning of this character for ocean: 洋. Sheep, being inland animals, graze on land away from the ocean; so water (氵) far away from the sheep (羊) came to mean ocean: 洋. By extension, 洋 also means "foreign", i.e., far away beyond the ocean.

`	`	氵	氵	氵	氵	洋	洋	洋							
1	2	3	4	5	6	7	8	9							

---

 huǒ
fire

火柴	huǒ chái	match
火车	huǒ chē	train
火光	huǒ guāng	flame; blaze
火海	huǒ hǎi	sea of fire
火花	huǒ huā	sparks
火化	huǒ huà	cremate
火箭	huǒ jiàn	rocket

火 is a pictograph of fire, produced by rubbing stones together. A terrifying force of nature, it brings both calamity and comfort to man. Like burning issues that often flare up in life, fire is easy to kindle, but difficult to handle, as the proverb warns: "you can't use paper to wrap up fire."

`	`	少	火												
1	2	3	4												

---

 yán
blaze;
flame

炎凉	yán liáng	cold-shoulder
炎热	yán rè	burning (or scorching) hot
炎夏	yán xià	hot summer
炎炎	yán yán	sweltering
炎症	yán zhèng	inflammation

The character for flame (炎) itself was formed from two fires (火), one atop the other. Because of its inflammatory nature, it may well spread like wildfire and the people around it would suffer from the burning heat.

`	`	少	火	火	火	炎	炎								
1	2	3	4	5	6	7	8								

zāi
calamity

灾害	zāi hài	calamity; disaster
灾患	zāi huàn	calamity
灾荒	zāi huāng	famine
灾祸	zāi huò	disaster
灾情	zāi qíng	condition of a disaster
灾区	zāi qū	disaster area

Man, plagued by floods (巛 , stream) and fire (火), once regarded these unforeseen calmities as divine judgement:(災). The modern simplified character for calamity: 灾 , however, sets matters straight by locating fire(火)under roof(宀) pinning the responsibility onto man himself.

丶	丷	宀	宀	灾	灾	灾					
1	2	3	4	5	6	7					

---

hēi
black

黑暗	hēi àn	dark
黑白	hēi bái	black and white
黑板	hēi bǎn	blackboard
黑人	hēi rén	black people
黑色	hēi sè	black
黑市	hēi shì	black market
黑夜	hēi yè	dark night

The original seal form depicted a flame(炎) under a smoke vent or window(田), blackening it(爨) with soot. Squaring the window: 田 and modifying the flame: 灬, produced the modern character: 黑 , meaning black.

丶	冂	冂	冂	四	甲	里	里	里	黑	黑	黑
1	2	3	4	5	6	7	8	9	10	11	12

---

mò
ink;
Chinese ink

墨迹	mò jì	ink mark
墨水	mò shuǐ	ink
墨砚	mò yàn	inkstone
墨鱼	mò yú	inkfish; cuttlefish
墨汁	mò zhī	prepared Chinese ink
墨水笔	mò shuǐ bǐ	fountain pen

Chinese ink: 墨 was first made by mixing smoke-soot (黑) with gum to produce and earthy(土) substance. The mixture was then moulded and hardened into a solid stick, ready to be ground with water to form live ink. Even though a little ink is better than a good memory, man apparently prefers to heed the proverb: "He who is near ink gets black," committing it to memory.

丶	冂	冂	冂	四	甲	里	里	里	黑	黑	黑	黑	墨	墨
1	2	3	4	5	6	7	8	9	10	11	12	13		15

英

yīng
brave;
heroic

英镑	yīng bàng	pound sterling
英豪	yīng háo	hero
英俊	yīng jùn	handsome
英明	yīng míng	brilliant
英名	yīng míng	illustrious name
英雄	yīng xióng	hero
英勇	yīng yǒng	courageous

A mature man (大) in the midst of a large space (冖), thick with vegetation (艹), suggests a brave man in a jungle. Hence: 英 , meaning brave or heroic. Although there will always be a brave man to respond to a high reward, the ancient saying reveals the true source of courage: "Men of principle have courage."

一 十 艹 艹 芐 苎 英 英
1 2 3 4 5 6 7 8

竹

zhú
bamboo

竹竿	zhú gān	bamboo pole
竹林	zhú lín	bamboo grove
竹笋	zhú sǔn	bamboo shoot
竹子	zhú zi	bamboo
山竹	shān zhú	mangosteen
竹叶青	zhú yè qīng	bamboo-leaf-green liqueur

Originally written: 𥫗, the character for bamboo is a pictograph of two whorls of bamboo leaves. Unlike a wayward man, the bamboo grows straight and up-right into a useful and decorative plant. "The bamboo stick makes a good child," so says the proverb. Our picture demonstrates how - starting right from the bottom.

丿 𠂉 𠂉 𥫗 竹 竹
1 2 3 4 5 6

笔

bǐ
pen;
pencil

笔记	bǐ jì	notes
笔迹	bǐ jì	writing
笔尖	bǐ jiān	pen nib
笔名	bǐ míng	pseudonym
笔墨	bǐ mò	pen and ink
笔误	bǐ wù	slip of the pen
笔战	bǐ zhàn	written polemics

A hand (彐) holding a stylus (丨), scratching lines (一) on a tablet (一), symbolizes a writting stylus: 聿. Bamboo (𥫗) added to stylus (聿) produces "pen": 筆. Bamboo (𥫗) combined with hair 毛 also makes "pen": 笔 . Although both the regular 笔 and simplified 筆 can be used to write "pen", the saying goes: "A pen cannot write two words at the same time."

丿 𠂉 𥫗 𥫗 竹 竹 笋 竿 竿 笔
1 2 3 4 5 6 7 8 9 10

笑 xiào
laugh; smile

笑话	xiào huà	joke
笑剧	xiào jù	farce
笑脸	xiào liǎn	smiling face
笑料	xiào liào	laughing-stock
笑骂	xiào mà	deride and taunt
笑容	xiào róng	smiling expression

笑 has an amusing origin. The phonetic element: 夭 depicts a man (大) inclining his head (丿) to laugh more easily, suggesting rocking or shaking. The radical component: ⺮ likens such laughter to the swaying of bamboo (⺮) in the breeze. But laughing or smiling is serious business, as implied in the proverb: "A man without a smiling face should not open a shop."

ノ	⺊	⺊	⺮	⺮	⺮	竺	竺	笭	笑
1	2	3	4	5	6	7	8	9	10

禾 hé
grain

禾叉	hé chā	pitchfork
禾虫	hé chóng	harvest grub
禾苗	hé miáo	grain seedling
禾黍	hé shǔ	millet
禾穗	hé suì	a ear (of rice grain)

禾, the radical for "grain", is a tree (木) with the top bent over to represent the head of a ripened grain. The grain-stalk provides, not only food for the body, but also food for thought: the more grain it bears in the head, the more it bends in humility.

一	二	千	禾	禾
1	2	3	4	5

秋 qiū
autumn

秋季	qiū jì	autumn season
秋千	qiū qiān	swing
秋色	qiū sè	autumn scenery
秋收	qiū shōu	autumn harvest
秋水	qiū shuǐ	autumn waters
秋天	qiū tiān	autumn
秋种	qiū zhòng	autumn sowing

During the autumn harvest, the grain (禾) ripens under the fiery heat (火) of the sun. Hence: 秋, meaning "autumn". In China, one can see the waste stalks of grain (禾) disposed of by fire (火) after the harvesting and threshing in Autumn.

一	二	千	禾	禾	禾	禾	秋	秋
1	2	3	4	5	6	7	8	9

愁 chóu
sad; melacholy

愁苦	chóu kǔ	anixety; distress
愁眉	chóu méi	knitted brows
愁闷	chóu mèn	feel gloomy
愁容	chóu róng	sorrowful countenance
愁绪	chóu xù	gloomy mood

As the year declines, with each falling leaf signalling autumn (秋), man's heart (心) becomes weighed down with a nostalgic melancholy: 愁. He realizes nature cannot jump from winter to summer without a spring or from summer to winter without a fall. Hence: 愁 - the influence of autumn(秋)on the heart (心).

丿	二	千	禾	禾	禾	秋	秋	秋	秋	愁	愁	愁						
1	2	3	4	5	6	7	8	9	10	11	12	13						

税 shuì
tax

税额	shuì é	amount of tax to be paid
税款	shuì kuǎn	tax payment; taxation
税率	shuì lǜ	tax rate
税收	shuì shōu	tax revenue
税制	shuì zhì	tax system

To justify taxation, man coined税from 禾 (grain) and 兑 (exchange). Evidently farmers paid their taxes in grain (禾) in "exchange" (兑) for services and privileges. The proverb, however, has the last word: "Those who are prospering do not argue about taxes." They just close their eyes, shut their mouths and pay through the nose.

丿	二	千	禾	禾	禾	秒	秒	秒	稅	稅	税							
1	2	3	4	5	6	7	8	9	10	11	12							

禿 tū
bald; bare

秃笔	tū bǐ	bald writing brush- (figuratively) poor writing ability
秃顶	tū dǐng	bald
秃山	tū shān	barren hill
秃头	tū tóu	bald head
秃子	tū zi	baldhead

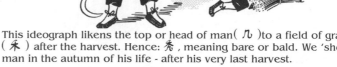

This ideograph likens the top or head of man(儿)to a field of grain (禾) after the harvest. Hence: 禿, meaning bare or bald. We 'show man in the autumn of his life - after his very last harvest.

丿	二	千	禾	禾	禾	禿												
1	2	3	4	5	6	7												

甘 gān
sweet

甘草	gān cǎo	licorice root
甘苦	gān kǔ	weal and woe
甘露	gān lù	sweet dew
甘心	gān xīn	willingly; readily
甘愿	gān yuàn	readily
甘蔗	gān zhe	sugarcane

"Sweetness" is handled with taste in the proverb: "All food tastes sweet to those who are hungry." The radical for "sweet" pictures the mouth（口）with something（一）in it worth holding - something sweet: 甘. 甘 can be extended to include anything pleasing to the senses, as illustrated here.

一	十	廿	廿	甘									
1	2	3	4	5									

牛 niú
ox; cow; bull

牛豆	niú dòu	cowpox
牛角	niú jiǎo	ox-horn
牛劲	niú jìn	great strength
牛奶	niú nǎi	milk
牛排	niú pái	beef steak
牛棚	niú péng	cowshed
牛肉	niú ròu	beef

The seal form of this character is a pictograph of the ox, characterized by two prominent horns: 牛. Man's slave for life, the cow or ox has been exploited to the bone for labour, meat, milk, leather, glue, manure, etc. Even the modern form: 牛 does not spare the poor animal its horn.

ノ	乞	二	牛										
1	2	3	4										

牢 láo
cattle pen; prison

牢固	láo gù	firm; secure
牢记	láo jì	remember well
牢牢	láo láo	firmly; safely
牢骚	láo sāo	grumbling; complaint
牢狱	láo yù	prison; jail
坐牢	zuò láo	be in prison

The seal form: pictures a paddock（口）confining an ox（牛）after the day's hard labour. The modern form: 牢 mercifully puts a roof（宀）over the beast（牛）. By extension, 牢 represents a prison for the incarceration of "beasts" of human society who are also in for "hard labour".

ノ	八	宀	宀	宀	空	牢							
1	2	3	4	5	6	7							

半 bàn
half

半岛	bàn dǎo	peninsula
半价	bàn jià	half-price
半票	bàn piào	half-price ticket
半生	bàn shēng	half a lifetime
半数	bàn shù	half the number
半天	bàn tiān	half of the day
半途	bàn tú	half way

This character originated from the butcher's practice of dividing (八) an ox (牛) into two halves, in all its length, before cutting up. 牛 was modified to 丰 to facilitate exact division. Hence: 半, meaning "half". Even though it is easy to split one ox into two halves, the saying proves true: "you cannot get two skins from one ox."

、	゛	゛	半	半					
1	2	3	4	5					

伴 bàn
companion; associate; mate

伴侣	bàn lǚ	companion; partner
伴随	bàn suí	accompany; follow
伴娘	bàn niáng	bridesmaid; maid-of-honour

The ideograph: 伴 is made up of man (亻) and half (半), suggesting that the single man is but half of a pair. To attain "oneness" another half, a complement, is needed. Hence: 伴, meaning companion, associate or mate. In the choice of a better half, let man take heed: "Tiger and deer do not walk together."

ノ	亻	亻	仏	仁	伫	伴			
1	2	3	4	5	6	7			

有 yǒu
have

有理	yǒu lǐ	reasonable
有力	yǒu lì	strong; powerful
有效	yǒu xiào	efficacious; valid
有利	yǒu lì	advantageous; favourable
有功	yǒu gōng	have rendered great service

Early forms portrayed a hand (ㅋ) grasping a piece of meat (夕), signifying to possess or to have: 有. Because of the resemblance between meat (夕) and moon (夕), man soon lost sight of meat and reached for the moon, promising it to anyone he wishes to possess. Today, with hand (ナ) on moon (月), he classified 有 under "moon".

一	ナ	才	有	有	有				
1	2	3	4	5	6				

来 lái
come

来宾	lái bīn	guest
来到	lái dào	arrive; come
来电	lái diàn	incoming telegram
来访	lái fǎng	come to visit
来回	lái huí	make a round trip
来客	lái kè	guest
来临	lái lín	approach; come

"He who sows his grain in the field puts his trust in heaven," so observed the proverb. A bountiful yield of grain was therefore gratefully acknowledged as having "come" from above. Thus 来, originally a pictograph of growing wheat or barley, came to stand for "come". The simplified form grafts rice (米) on to tree (木) to produce 来 - a character no less welcome.

一	一	一	一	平	来	来					
1	2	3	4	5	6	7					

果 guǒ
fruit

果断	guǒ duàn	resolute; decisive
果酱	guǒ jiàng	jam
果皮	guǒ pí	skin of fruit
果品	guǒ pǐn	fruit
果肉	guǒ ròu	flesh of fruit
果实	guǒ shí	fruit; gain
果树	guǒ shù	fruit tree

The earliest form was a stylised tree sporting a showy display of fruit: . As it grew mighty, it boasted of more fruit: but these are not easily discernible in the modern form: 果 . The proverb provides a clue to the missing fruit: "Though a tree grows to a thousand feet, its fruits will fall to earth again."

丶	口	曰	日	旦	甲	畀	果				
1	2	3	4	5	6	7	8				

课 kè
lesson

课本	kè běn	textbook
课程	kè chéng	course; curriculum
课外	kè wài	outside class
课文	kè wén	text
课余	kè yú	after school
功课	gōng kè	homework
上课	shàng kè	attend class

課, meaning "lesson", is based on words(言)and fruit(果). A lesson(课) involves the use of words of instruction (言) to produce results, i.e., bear fruit(果). But, for words to be fruitful, take a lesson from the proverb: bitter words are medicine; sweet words bring illness."

丶	讠	讠	讠	讠	讠	讠	课	课	课		
1	2	3	4	5	6	7	8	9	10		

未 wèi

not;
not yet

未必	wèi bì	not necessarily
未曾	wèi céng	have not; never
未定	wèi dìng	uncertain; undecided
未婚	wèi hūn	unmarried
未来	wèi lái	future
未完	wèi wán	unfinished

This character is to be distinguished from 末 (limit) in that the horizontal stroke across the top is much shorter: 未. In 末 the top line is emphasized; in 未 it is subdued, not fully grown. Hence 未: not yet. Those who have "not yet" attained their end should exercise patience and take heart from the proverb: "A giant tree grows from a tiny bud."

一	二	十	才	未						
1	2	3	4	5						

妹 mèi

younger
sister

妹夫	mèi fū	younger sister's husband
妹妹	mèi mei	younger sister
表妹	biǎo mèi	younger female cousin

未, the phonetic, is a tree in full leaf and branch, but not fully mature and means: "not". With the addition of the radical for girl (女), the character for "younger sister' is formed. Hence 妹: a girl (女) who has not yet (未) reached maturity.

㇜	女	女	女ノ	女二	妹	妹	妹			
1	2	3	4	5	6	7	8			

姐 jiě

elder
sister

姐夫	jiě fū	elder sister's husband
姐姐	jiě jie	elder sister
姐妹	jiě mèi	sisters
表姐	biǎo jiě	elder female cousin

女 is the radical for girl or woman. 且, the phonetic, is a picture of a stool (冂) with two rungs (二), standing on the ground (一), now borrowed for the conjunction: 且 "moreover". In our picture, the stool is not the only thing that distinguishes older sister from younger sister.

㇜	女	女	姐	姐	姐	姐	姐			
1	2	3	4	5	6	7	8			

爱 ài
love; affection

爱国	ài guó	patriotic
爱好	ài hào	interest; hobby
爱护	ài hù	cherish; take good care of
爱怜	ài lián	show tender affection for
爱惜	ài xī	treasure; cherish

The regular form: 愛 is made up of 爫 (breathe into), 心 (heart) and 夂 (gracious motion), implying that what gives breath to the heart and inspires gracious motion is love - an idealistic love. The simplifed form: 爱 highlights the role of friendship: 友 (hand ナ in hand 又 co-operation) - a more realistic love. But whatever form love may take, none can excel the selfless and unselfish love based on the principle extolled in the proverb: "Those who love others will themselves be loved."

一	丶	亠	丷	亚	爫	兕	严	旁	爱
1	2	3	4	5	6	7	8	9	10

想 xiǎng
think; hope

想到	xiǎng dào	think of; call to mind
想来	xiǎng lái	it may be assumed that
想念	xiǎng niàn	remember with longing; miss
想起	xiǎng qǐ	recall

This character is composed of 相 (inspect) and 心 (heart). The phonetic: li represents an eye (目) behind a tree (木) on the lookout for possible danger, and signifies to examine or inspect. Combination with the radical: 心 (heart, mind) produces 想, meaning to examine or inspect in the heart or mind, i.e., to think, ponder or hope.

一	十	才	木	木	机	相	相	相	相	想	想	想
1	2	3	4	5	6	7	8	9	10	11	12	13

忆 yì
recall; remember; reflect

回忆	huí yì	recollect
记忆	jì yì	remember
记忆力	jì yì lì	memory

The phonetic: 意 denotes sound (音) in the heart or mind (心), i.e., intention or thought. The addition of another heart (the radical 忄) to thought (意) suggests to think again - to reflect or remember: 憶 . As a mnemonic aid, the simplified form combines heart (忄) with second (乙) producing 忆 .

丶	小	忄	忆
1	2	3	4

忘 wàng
forget

忘本	wàng běn	forget one's origin
忘掉	wàng diào	forget
忘怀	wàng huái	forget
忘记	wàng jì	forget
忘情	wàng qíng	be unmoved
忘我	wàng wǒ	selfless
忘形	wàng xíng	be beside oneself

The old form of the phonetic: 亡 represents someone entering (入) a place of concealment (乚), and means to disappear or perish: (亾). The addition of the heart radical: 心 enforces the idea of "lost mind" or a mind that ceases to act; hence, to forget: 忘. Minds should not be lost when it comes to the memorable proverb: "Forget favours given: remember favours received."

丶	亠	亡	广	忘	忘	忘								
1	2	3	4	5	6	7								

聪 cōng
intelligent; clever

聪慧	cōng huì	bright; intelligent
聪明	cōng míng	intelligent
聪颖	cōng yǐng	bright; clever

This character enlarges on 悤 (excitement, haste) by adding the ear radical (耳) to produce, suggesting quickness at hearing or grasping ideas, i.e., intelligent. The simplified form ingeniously combines 耳 (ear) with 总 (general, comprehensive) to convey the idea of cleverness at hearing and comprehending things generally: 聪.

一	厂	厂	耳	耳	耳	耳	耵	耵	耶	聍	聕	聪	聪	聪
1	2	3	4	5	6	7	8	9	10	11	12	13	14	15

慧 huì
wit; wisdom

慧心	huì xīn	wisdom
慧眼	huì yǎn	mental discernment
智慧	zhì huì	wisdom

Two leafy branches (丰丰) held in the hand (ヨ) improvise a broom (彗). Broom (彗) placed over heart (心) clears the way for wit and wisdom. Hence: 慧 - a heart swept clean, ready to receive the proverbial counsel: "Man combs his hair every morning; why not his heart?"

一	⺀	三	丰	丰	丰	丰	拝	彗	彗	彗	彗	慧	慧	慧
1	2	3	4	5	6	7	8	9	10	11	12	13	14	15

恶

ě, è or wù
evil

恶毒	è dú	malicious
恶化	è huà	worsen
恶劣	è liè	harsh; abominable
恶习	è xí	bad habits
恶心	ě xīn	nauseating
恶意	è yì	ill-will
可恶	kě wù	hateful

In the phonetic: 亚 (ugly), the vertical line is double to indicate imperfection and deformity. The two horizontal lines （二） signify second or inferior. Pictographically, 亚 suggests two hunchbacks facing each other, representing ugliness. 亚 (ugliness) collaborates with the heart （心） to breed evil: 恶, stirring up in the mind the proverbial exhortation: "See no evil; hear no evil; speak no evil; and do no evil."

一	丆	丌	开	亚	亚	亚	恶	恶	恶					
1	2	3	4	5	6	7	8	9	10					

恩

ēn
mercy;
kindness;
grace

恩爱	ēn ài	conjugal love; loving
恩德	ēn dé	kindness; grace
恩典	ēn diǎn	favour; grace
恩惠	ēn huì	favour; kindness
恩情	ēn qíng	loving-kindness
恩人	ēn rén	benefactor

Why is a mature man （大） confined in a cell or enclosure（口）? The answer forms the character: 囚, meaning cause or reason. The sight of such a confined man may excite pity in the heart （心）, and if this feeling leads one to liberate him, that is grace or mercy - the result of tempering reason （因） with sentiment （心）.

丨	冂	冃	冈	因	因	因	恩	恩	恩					
1	2	3	4	5	6	7	8	9	10					

合

hé
unite;
join

合唱	hé chàng	chorus
合法	hé fǎ	legal; lawful
合格	hé gé	qualified; up to standard
合伙	hé huǒ	form a partnership
合计	hé jì	add up to; amount to; total

The upper portion of this character is made up of three lines joined together to form a balanced triangle: 亼, indicating "together". The lower part is the character for "mouth": 口. Hence: 合 - three mouths （口） together （亼）, i.e., unity and understanding - a very rare occurrence, as the saying goes: "If three persons can agree entirely, then the earth can be changed to gold."

丿	人	亼	合	合	合									
1	2	3	4	5	6									

佥 qiān
unanimous;
all together

佥谋	qiān móu	plan decided by all
佥议	qiān yì	public opinion

佥 is a coming together (亼) of mouth (吅) sand persons (从). 亼 signifies together; indicates the clamour of voices; and 从 represents persons, one following another. 佥 therefore means unanimous or all together. Coincidentally, 佥 bears a striking resemblance to the face in a crowd and, clarified by the flsh radical (月), stands for face: 臉.

ノ	人	亼	佥	佥	佥	佥						
1	2	3	4	5	6	7						

今 jīn
now;
present

今后	jīn hòu	from now on
今年	jīn nián	this year
今天	jīn tiān	today
今生	jīn shēng	this life
今昔	jīn xī	the present and the past

This character, dealing with time, is composed of 亼 and フ (contraction of 及). 亼 shows the continuity of the time and unity of its three elements: past, present and future. 及 (or フ) is a hand (又) holding a person (人), suggesting contact. Hence: 今, the time element we are always in contact with - the present.

ノ	人	亼	今									
1	2	3	4									

念 niàn
read;
recite

念经	niàn jīng	recite or chant scriptures
念头	niàn tóu	thought
念珠	niàn zhū	beads; rosary
观念	guān niàn	sense; idea; concept
怀念	huái niàn	cherish

The components of 念 are 今 (present) and 心 (Heart). 念 is to bring the mind the past - by means of reading, reciting or chanting. Derived meanings include thinking, studying, remembering and even wishing to revive the past.

ノ	人	亼	今	今	念	念	念					
1	2	3	4	5	6	7	8					

贪 tān
covet; greedy

贪婪	tān lán	avaricious; greedy
贪图	tān tú	covet
贪污	tān wū	corruption
贪心	tān xīn	greedy
贪脏	tān zāng	take bribes; practise graft
贪便宜	tān pián yi	keep on gaining petty advantages

The presence（今）of anything precious（贝, cowrie money) arouses the emotion of covetousness or greed. Hence: 贪, to covet. Such greed enables a person to gain the things money can but and lose the things money cannot but.

ノ	人	𠆢	今	今	含	贪	贪							
1	2	3	4	5	6	7	8							

金 jīn
gold; metal

金融	jīn róng	finance
金色	jīn sè	golden
金鱼	jīn yú	goldfish
白金	bái jīn	platinum
黄金	huáng jīn	gold
金字塔	jīn zì tǎ	pyramid

The original seal form: 金 showed the presence（今）of four gold nugget（㸆）hidden in the earth（土）. The regular form reveals only two nuggets: 金. In the simplified radical form, even these two remaining nuggets are missing: 钅. However, the proverb reassures us: "True gold fears no fire." Only thieves!

ノ	人	𠆢	今	全	全	金	金							
1	2	3	4	5	6	7	8							

银 yín
silver

银杯	yín bēi	silver cup; trophy
银币	yín bì	silver coin
银行	yín háng	bank
银河	yín hé	the Milky Way (sky)
银婚	yín hūn	silver wedding
银幕	yín mù	(motion-picture) screen

Silver is produced by consolidating 金 (gold) with 艮 (hard): 银. 艮, originally the eye（目）turned suddenly around（匕）to look a man full in the face defiantly, means "obstinate". Compared with gold, silver is a hard（艮）metal（金）, more precious than common copper. Hence the saying: "Even he who has accumulated 10,000 taels of silver cannot take with him at death half a copper?"

ノ	𠂆	𠂉	𠂹	钅	钅	钅	钽	钽	银	银				
1	2	3	4	5	6	7	8	9	10	11				

钱 qián
money

钱币	qián bì	coin
钱包	qián bāo	wallet; purse
钱财	qián cái	wealth
捐钱	juān qián	donate money
零钱	líng qián	small change
赚钱	zhuàn qián	earn money

Two spears 戋 breaking gold（金）into pieces means "money": 钱. And money, taking on the vicious character of spears, means power. So, when money talks, man listens in silence and whispers: "If you are rich, you speak the truth; if you are poor, your words are but lies."

ノ	⼁	⻓	⻓	金	钅	钅	钱	钱	钱					
1	2	3	4	5	6	7								

针 zhēn
needle

针对	zhēn duì	directed at
针灸	zhēn jiǔ	acupuncture
针线	zhēn xiàn	needlework
针眼	zhēn yǎn	the eye of a needle
针织	zhen zhī	knitting
打针	dǎ zhēn	an injection

This character was originally written: 針, comprising 金 (metal) and 咸 (bite). The needle takes up, as it were, mouthfuls of cloth, biting its way along. The regular form 钊 has a good point, with the substituted phonetic 十 resembling a threaded needle - warning us never to bite off more than we can chew, for "No needle is sharp at both ends."

ノ	⼁	⻓	⻓	金	钅	针								
1	2	3	4	5	6	7								

钉 dīng
nail

钉锤	dīng chuí	hammer
钉帽	dīng mào	the head of a nail
钉耙	dīng pá	(iron-toothed) rake
钉鞋	dīng xié	spiked shoes
钉子	dīng zi	nail

Originally, this character was a pictograph of a nail: 丁. Clarified with the metal radical（金）, it is now written 釘 and simplified to 钉. 丁 itself now stands for a strong male adult or soldier for, in a sense, nails are soldiers - strong, useful but never really valued. Hence the saying: "Use not good iron to make nails, nor good men soldiers."

ノ	⼁	⻓	⻓	金	钅	钉								
1	2	3	4	5	6	7								

户 hù
door

户口	hù kǒu	household; (bank) account
户外	hù wài	outdoor
户主	hù zhǔ	head of a family
住户	zhù hù	occupants

户 is a pictograph of a one-leafed door, and constitues the radical part of numerous characters relating to doors and spaces. It is also symbolic of the house and family, the hinge of the ancient door was a vertical beam acting as a pivot; and because of its constant movement and workload, it was cited as an example in the saying: "The hinge of a door is never crowded with insects."

丶　ㄱ　ㄋ　户
1　2　3　4

方 fāng
square

方便	fāng biàn	convenient
方法	fāng fǎ	method; way
方格	fāng gé	checks
方略	fāng lüè	general plan
方向	fāng xiàng	direction
方形	fāng xíng	square
方言	fāng yán	dialect

The original version was a graphic representation of two boats lashed together to form a square barge ▯:. This was replaced by the symbol: ᛉ, indicating the four regions of a square with two dimensions, i.e., the earthly surface. Modified to ᛉ and finally 方, it widened its scope to mean also region, direction and even upright, or puritanical.

丶　一　亠　方
1　2　3　4

房 fáng
room; house

房产	fáng chǎn	house property
房顶	fáng dǐng	roof
房基	fáng jī	foundations (of a building)
房间	fáng jiān	room
房客	fáng kè	tenant; lodger
房契	fáng qì	title deed

房 combines 户 (door) with 方 (square). It indicates something squarish (方) with a door (户), i.e., a house or a room. Viewing house and room squarely, one preverb draws the conclusion: "Even though your dwelling contains a thousand rooms, you can use but eight feet of space a night."

丶　ㄱ　ㄋ　户　户　户　房　房
1　2　3　4　5　6　7　8

斤 jīn
kati

斤两	jīn liǎng	weight
斤斤计较	jīn jīn jì jiào	be calculating
半斤八两	bàn jīn bā liǎng	not much to choose between the two

斤 is a pictograph of an axe. Originally meaning "axe", it eventually became a standard measure of weight - a kati - probably because the ancient balance weight or counterpoise was shaped like an axe-head. Handling the axe with skill to produce results requires initiative and personal effort - the point of the saying: "The axe strikes the chisel; and the chisel strikes the wood."

´	厂	斤	斤				
1	2	3	4				

所 suǒ
place

所得	suǒ dé	income; earnings
所谓	suǒ wèi	what is called; so-called
所以	suǒ yǐ	so; therefore; as a result
所有	suǒ yǒu	own; possess
所在	suǒ zài	place; location

所 is a juxtaposition of 尸 (door) and 斤 (axe), and refers to the place where fuel is prepared. In olden times, the shopping of firewood with the axe (斤) was done near the door or house (尸). Hence: 所 (axe beside house) meaning place or location.

´	厂	斥	户	斤	所	所	所
1	2	3	4	5	6	7	8

匠 jiàng
artisan; craftsman

匠人	jiàng rén	artisan; craftsman
匠心	jiàng xīn	ingenuity; craftsmanship
木匠	mù jiàng	carpenter
石匠	shí jiàng	stonemason
铁匠	tiě jiàng	blacksmith

An arlsan: 匠 is represented by his tool: 斤 (an axe) and his work: 匚 (a hollowed-out log, vessel or box). The craftsman's dependence upon his tools prompts the saying: "The workman who would do his work well should first sharpen his tools."

一	二	厂	尸	斤	匠
1	2	3	4	5	6

兵 bīng
soldier; army

兵变	bīng biàn	mutiny
兵器	bīng qì	arms
兵役	bīng yì	military service
兵营	bīng yíng	barracks
步兵	bù bīng	infantry
工兵	gōng bīng	engineer (soldier)
士兵	shì bīng	soldier

兵 is represented by two hands (屮 or 廾) brandishing a battle-axe (斤) - symbol of the soldier. Lamenting the necessity of maintaining an army in a belligerent world, one proverb concludes: "Feed soldiers for a thousand days, to be used for one day."

ノ	┌	┌	斤	丘	乒	兵							
1	2	3	4	5	6	7							

近 jìn
near

近海	jìn hǎi	coastal waters
近乎	jìn hū	close to
近况	jìn kuàng	recent development
近来	jìn lái	recently
近邻	jìn lín	neighbour
近亲	jìn qīn	close relatives

This ideograph suggests the proper way for a warrior to advance(乚) to battle - with battle-axe 斤 in hand, i.e., near. Hence: 近, meaning "near". The ideograph for "far": 遠 combines 乚 (proceed or walk) with 袁 (a long robe, necessary for a long journey).

ノ	┌	斤	斤	沂	近								
1	2	3	4	5	6								

质 zhì
character; quality

质地	zhì dì	texture
质料	zhì liào	material
质问	zhì wèn	question
质疑	zhì yí	query
本质	běn zhì	innate character
品质	pǐn zhì	quality; character
人质	rén zhì	hostage

Two axes, (斦) poised above a cowrie shell (貝), representing something precious), are ready to dissect it and ascertain its worth: 質. The axes ensure a complete and thorough job. Hence: 質, denoting value, quality, nature or character.

一	┌	厂	斤	斦	所	质	质						
1	2	3	4	5	6	7	8						

新 xīn
new

新兵	xīn bīng	new recruit
新婚	xīn hūn	newly-married
新郎	xīn láng	bridgegroom
新年	xīn nián	New Year
新娘	xīn niáng	bridge
新奇	xīn qí	strange; new; novel
新闻	xīn wén	news

Rods, freshly chopped from the hazel bush (亲) for flexibility, were once used for flogging criminals, sometimes to extort a confession. Hence: 新 , the symbol for "new", indicated by the hazel rods (亲) and the axe (斤).

﹀	二	亠	立	辛	亲	亲	亲	新	新	新
1	2	3	4	5	6	7	8	9	10	11	12	13

门 mén
door; gate

门第	mén dì	family status
门户	mén hù	door
门槛	mén kǎn	threshold
门口	mén kǒu	doorway
门牌	mén pái	house number
门徒	mén tú	disciple
门诊	mén zhěn	outpatient service

Just as 户 symbolises a one-leafed door, so 門 represents a door with two leaves. Doors provide exits and entrances, but not all are convenient, as exemplified in the proverb: "The door of charity is hard to open, and hard to shut." To simplify matters, the regular door: 門 has now been stripped down to an open doorway: 门 .

﹀	冂	门
1	2	3

们 mén
plural sign

你们	nǐ men	you (second person plural)
人们	rén men	people; the public
他们	tā men	they; them
我们	wǒ men	we; us

This character has 人 (person) as radical and 門 (door) as phonetic. 門 is a door with two leaves instead of one (as in 户). Clarified by the radical for person (人), it is the plural sign for nouns and pronouns, applied to people: 們 .

ノ	亻	亻	仆	们
1	2	3	4	5

问 wèn
ask;
enquire;
question

问答	wèn dá	questions and answers
问号	wèn hào	question mark
问候	wèn hòu	extend greetings to someone
问世	wèn shì	be published; come out
问讯	wèn xùn	inquire; ask

Enquires are often made at the door, the entrance to a house. A mouth（口）at the door（門）therefore becomes a fitting ideograph for ask or enquire: 問. It can also mean question or interrogate, although to do so in an officious manner would be, according to the saying, "asking the blind man the way." （问道于盲）

` 丶 亅 门 门 问 问

1 2 3 4 5 6

闻 wén
hear;
news

闻名	wén míng	famous
闻人	wén rén	celebrity
丑闻	chǒu wén	scandal
新闻	xīn wén	news
要闻	yào wén	important news

In this ideograph, "ear"（耳）becomes "hear"（聞）when placed at the door（門）. By extension 闻 also means news", for the ear （耳）is the door（門）of knowledge or information. But not all news obtained by the ear is reliable, as the saying goes: "What the ear hears is not equal to what the eye sees."

` 丶 亅 门 门 闩 闫 闻 闻

1 2 3 4 5 6 7 8 9

开 kāi
open

开办	kāi bàn	set up; establish
开采	kāi cǎi	mine; extract
开除	kāi chú	expel
开动	kāi dòng	start
开端	kāi duān	beginning
开始	kāi shǐ	start
公开	gōng kāi	open (adj)

A bar or bolt（一）across the door（門）means to shut 閂. Two hands（廾）taking away the bar（一）signifies to open: 開. But there is more to the business of opening than just unbolting the door. As the proverb says: "To open a shop is easy; the difficult thing is to keep it open."

一 二 于 开

1 2 3 4

富 fù

rich; abundant

富丽	fù lì	grand; magnificent
富强	fù qiáng	prosperous and strong
富饶	fù ráo	bountiful; fertile
富庶	fù shù	rich and abundant
富翁	fù wēng	wealthy man
富裕	fù yù	wealthy

Man created this symbol for material prosperity: 富 from 宀 (roof), 高 (high) and 田 (field). Under shelter of the roof (宀), he piled up high (高 or 畐) the products of his field (田) and amassed great wealth: 富. Spiritual wealth, however, is to he preferred, according to the saying: "Riches adorn the house; virtue adorns the person."

宝 bǎo

precious

宝贝	bǎo bèi	treasured object; baby
宝贵	bǎo guì	valuable; precious
宝剑	bǎo jiàn	a double-edged sword
宝库	bǎo kù	treasure-house
宝物	bǎo wù	treasure

Among the ancients, the precious things under the roof (宀) were jade (玉 or 王), earthenware (缶) and money cowrie (貝). Hence: 寶, meaning precious. Under his roof, modern man treasures sures gem or jade (玉), so he simplified 寶 to 宝. But, in his shop, "customers are the precious things; goods are only grass."

害 hài

harm; injure

害虫	hài chóng	harmful insect
害处	hài chù	harm
害怕	hài pà	afraid
害臊	hài sào	feel ashamed
害羞	hài xiū	bashful; shy
除害	chú hài	eliminate evil
利害	lì hài	terrible; formidable

丰 represents a stick (丨) marred by notches (彡); mouth (口) suggests harm caused by slander; and roof (宀) indicates injury done under cover, i.e., secretly. From these components man created harm: 害, fully realising that `he who harms others, harms himself" (害人反害己)

55

定 **dìng**
fix;
decide;
certain

定单	dìng dān	order form
定购	dìng gòu	order
定婚	dìng hūn	be engaged
定价	dìng jià	fixed price
定居	dìng jū	settle down
定理	dìng lǐ	theorem
否定	fǒu dìng	deny; negative

This character is made up of roof (宀) and order (正 or 疋). It signifies peace and order under the roof, implanting the idea of fixed, certain or decided: 定. Order under the roof comes before order under the heavens, although the proverb states in no uncertain terms: "is for man to plan, but for Heaven to decide."

丶	丷	宀	宀	宁	宇	庄	定				
1	2	3	4	5	6	7	8				

完 **wán**
finish;
complete

完备	wán bèi	complete
完毕	wán bì	finish; complete
完成	wán chéng	accomplish; complete
完稿	wán gǎo	complete the manuscript
完美	wán měi	perfect, flawless

This ideograph places roof (宀) over head (元). 元 means that which is upon (上 or 二) a person (人 or 儿), i.e., the head, origin or principle. So, putting on the roof(宀) over the head(元)finishes (完) the building. Hence: 完 , the end.

丶	丷	宀	宀	宁	宇	完					
1	2	3	4	5	6	7					

刀 **dāo**
knife

刀叉	dāo chā	knife and fork
刀架	dāo jià	tool carrier
刀具	dāo jù	cutting tool; tool
刀片	dāo piàn	razor blade
刀鞘	dāo qiào	sheath; scabbard
刀子	dāo zi	small knife; pocketknife

This radical is a pictograph of a knife or sword. Wielded in the cause of justice, the sword protects the innocent; but brandished irresponsibly, it is double-edged. A sharp blade is likened to a person vested with too much power, and a proverb warns: "A knife that's too sharp easily cuts the fingers."

刁	刀										
1	2										

fēn
divide;
separate

分别	fēn bié	differentiate
分布	fēn bù	be distributed
分界	fēn jiè	boundary
分开	fēn kāi	separate; part
分类	fēn lèi	classify
分裂	fēn liè	split; break up
分配	fēn pèi	distribute; allot

This ideograph is made up of 八 (divide), and clarified by radical 刀 (knife) to enforce the idea of dividing or separating: 八. It is like dividing (八) with a knife (刀). 分 is used also for any small division, component or part, e.g., a minute, a mark or a cent.

ノ	八	分	分							
1	2	3	4							

gōng
strength;
force;
power

弓箭	gōng jiàn	bow and arrow
弓弦	gōng xián	bowstring
弓形	gōng xíng	arch-shaped

弓 is a radical representing a Chinese bow: B. The ancient form shows It bent or vibrating: 㠱. Drawing the string (|) of the bow (弓) produces the character 引 , meaning to pull, guide or introduce. Though the bow is a lethal weapon for offence and defence, the proverb counsels: "Draw your bow, but don't shoot."

ㄱ	ㄱ	弓								
1	2	3								

fú
not;
no

自愧弗如	zì kuì fú rú	feel ashamed of one's inferiority

This character is both pictographic and ideographic. It depicts two divergent rod ( )( ) so tied together with a coil of rope (弓) that their forces are neutralised suggesting opposition or negation; hence the meaning "not": 弗 .

ㄱ	ㄱ	弓	弗	弗						
1	2	3	4	5						

费 fèi
expenses; squander

费力	fèi lì	strenuous
费时	fèi shí	time-consuming
费用	fèi yòng	expenses
会费	huì fèi	membership dues
浪费	làng fèi	waste; squander
免费	miǎn fèi	free of charge
学费	xué fèi	school fees

The phonetic: 弗, representing two rods bent in opposite directions being bound together, means "not". 贝 is a picture of a cowrie shell, once used as money. 弗 placed over 贝 therefore signifies under-valuing money, by inference, to waste or squander: 费.

一	一	弓	弓	弗	弗	弗	费	费			
1	2	3	4	5	6	7	8	9			

剃 tì
shave

剃刀	tì dāo	razor
剃度	tì dù	tonsure
剃头	tì tóu	haircutting

剃 combines 弟 (younger brother) with 刂 (knife or razor). 弟, the phonetic, depicts a thread round a spindle and means, by extension, a succession of brothers or younger brothers. The growing hair is suggested by the thread being unwound from the spindle (弟), and the addition of the razor (刂) gives us the character for shave: 剃. Our picture, however, shows how younger brother (弟) and razor (刂), put together, can mean a close shave.

丶	丷	丷	兰	弓	弟	弟	弟	剃			
1	2	3	4	5	6	7	8	9			

矢 shǐ
arrow

矢量	shǐ liàng	vector
飞矢	fēi shǐ	flying arrow
风矢	fēng shǐ	wind vector

The arrow radical, in its original form: 朱, bears a striking resemblance to an arrow with full tip and feathers. It was later modified to 矢 and finally stylised: 矢. Emphasizing the difficulty of combating insidious enemies, the saying goes: "It is easy to dodge a spear in the open, but difficult to avoid an arrow shot from hiding." (明枪易挡，暗箭难防。)

丿	𠂉	𠂊	午	矢							
1	2	3	4	5							

知 zhī
know

知道	zhī dào	know
知底	zhī dǐ	know the inside story
知己	zhī jǐ	bosom friend
知交	zhī jiāo	bosom friend
知觉	zhī jué	consciousness
知名	zhī míng	well-known
知识	zhī shi	knowledge

The radical: 矢 (arrow) represents swiftness. Combined with 口 (mouth), it means knowledge（知）, possessed by one who can give his word or opinion with the precision and speed of an arrow （矢）. Knowledge（知）is having a mouth（口）that is as sharp and far-reaching as an arrow（矢）. Unfortunately, according to the proverb, "Those who know much talk little; those who know little talk much."（知者不言，言者不知）

ノ	㇄	㇒	矢	矢	矢	知	知
1	2	3	4	5	6	7	8

医 yī
cure; heal

医生	yī shēng	doctor
医术	yī shù	medical treatment
医药	yī yào	medicine
医院	yī yuàn	hospital
医治	yī zhì	cure; treat
军医	jūn yī	medical officer (in the army)

Ancient man attribute sickness to evil influences. Healing: 醫, therefore, was symbolised by drawing arrows from the quiver （醫）to shoot（殳）at the demon of disease. Wine（酉）was indispensable as an elixir. Although the modern form of healing is very much simplified: 医, the saying still goes: "A wise doctor never treats himself."

一	厂	匚	三	至	矢	医
1	2	3	4	5	6	7

丑 chǒu
shameful; ugly

丑恶	chǒu è	ugly; repulsive
丑化	chǒu huà	smear; defame
丑角	chǒu jué	clown
丑陋	chǒu lòu	ugly
丑事	chǒu shì	scandal
丑态	chǒu tài	ugly performance

Two types of spirits were integrated to form the character for shame and ugliness: spirit or liquor （酉）from a wine jar, and an evil spirit（鬼）from the invisible realm. The result is a hideous drunken（酉）devil（鬼）or 醜, representing ugliness, now hidden under the simplified form: 丑 of a clown.

了	刀	丑	丑
1	2	3	4

狗 gǒu
dog

狗熊	gǒu xióng	black bear
海狗	hǎi gǒu	fur seal; ursine seal
狗腿子	gǒu tuǐ zi	hired thug; lackey; henchman

This character for dog: 狗 fittingly combines the dog radical:犭 (or 犬) with the phonetic: 句·勾, meaning a sentence of words, suggests barking - a distinguishing characteristic of the dog. Counselling against the thoughtless ill-treatment of the underdog, the proverb warns: "In beating a dog, first find out who the owner is."

ノ	丿	犭	犭	狗	狗	狗	狗						
1	2	3	4	5	6	7	8						

猴 hóu
monkey

In ancient times, skill in archery was the basis for selecting officials. In man (亻), precision in shooting an arrow (矢) at a target (厂 or コ) represented uprightness of heart. Hence the derived meaning of nobleman or prince: 侯. The addition of the animal radical:犭 extends the meaning to: "Prince among animals," a title applicable to the noble monkey: 猴. Featured here is the King of Monkeys, legendary hero of the classic: "Journey to the West."

猴戏	hóu xì	monkey show
猴子	hóu zi	monkey

ノ	丿	犭	犭	犭	犭	犭	犭	犭	猴	猴	猴		
1	2	3	4	5	6	7	8	9	10	11	12		

吠 fèi
bark

狗吠	gǒu fèi	bark of dogs

Mouth (口) plus dog (犬) equals bark: 吠. This character, therefore, shows what makes a dog bark. The ancient proverb, however, explains what makes a hundred dogs bark: "One dog barks at something, and a hundred bark at the sound."

丨	口	口	口	吠	吠	吠							
1	2	3	4	5	6	7							

狱 yù
prison; jail

狱吏	yù lì	prison officer; jailer
狱卒	yù zú	prison guard
地狱	dì yù	hell
监狱	jiān yù	prison
入狱	rù yù	be imprisoned
越狱	yuè yù	escape from prison

This ideograph places speech (言) between two different forms of dogs (犭and 犬). It represents a lawsuit: 獄, with the two suitors barking at each other like dogs. 獄 also means prison - for the loser. And, for the winner: "Win your lawsuit, and lose your money."

ノ	丬	犭	犭	犲	犲	狱	狱	狱			
1	2	3	4	5	6	7	8	9			

哭 kū
cry; wail; weep

哭泣	kū qì	cry; weep
哭诉	kū sù	complain tearfully

This character uses two mouths(口口) to express intense action of the mouth, resembling the wailing of dogs (犬); so dog (犬) with two mouths(口口) means "wail": 哭. Two mouths may effectively express crying and howling, but certainly, "two buckets of tears," according to the proverb, "will not heal a bruise."

丶	丷	口	吅	吅	叩	哭	哭	哭	哭		
1	2	3	4	5	6	7	8	9	10		

伏 fú
prostrate

伏安	fú ān	volt-ampere
伏兵	fú bīng	(troops in) ambush
伏法	fú fǎ	be executed
伏击	fú jī	ambush
伏贴	fú tiē	fit perfectly

This ideograph reduces man (亻) to the level of the lowly dog (犬). It means: "Man behaving like dog," prostrating himself or humiliating another: 伏. The saying proves true: "Flog the cur that's fallen into the water" - be merciless to bad people.

ノ	亻	亻	仕	伏	伏						
1	2	3	4	5	6						

突 tū
suddenly

突变	tū biàn	sudden change
突破	tū pò	break through
突起	tū qǐ	break out; rise high
突然	tū rán	suddenly
突兀	tū wù	lofty (landscape); sudden
突袭	tū xí	surprise attack

穴 is a hole made by removing and dividing (八) rock or earth to provide a roof (宀) over the wild dog's head. 突 represents the dog (犬) rushing out of its den (穴) to attack and bite an intruder. Hence the meaning suddenly or unexpectedly - without warning, as the saying goes: "A biting dog does not show its teeth."

丶	八	宀	宀	穴	空	宨	突	突
1	2	3	4	5	6	7	8	9

狂 kuáng
mad;
wild;
eccentric

狂暴	kuáng bào	violent
狂吠	kuáng fèi	bark furiously
狂风	kuáng fēng	fierce wind
狂热	kuáng rè	fanaticism
狂人	kuáng rén	maniac
狂喜	kuáng xǐ	wild with joy
狂笑	kuáng xiào	laugh wildly

王, the phonetic, is a contraction of 生, meaning luxuriant vegetation that sprouts (生) from the earth (土) and grows wild, indicating a rambling nature. 狂, therefore, is like a mad dog that strays or roams about aimlessly (王), suggesting the meaning: "mad or wild." Instead of advocating madness against madness, the proverb recommends prevention rather than cure: "If the fence is secure, no dog will enter."

丿	犭	犭	犭	狂	狂	狂
1	2	3	4	5	6	7

犯 fàn
transgress;
violate;
offend

犯法	fàn fǎ	violate the law
犯规	fàn guī	break the rules
犯忌	fàn jì	violate a taboo
犯人	fàn rén	convict
犯疑	fàn yí	suspect; be suspicious
犯罪	fàn zuì	commit a crime

The phonetic: 巳 means to blossom, sprout, expand or erupt. Dog (犭) with blossom (巳) - like dog in a flower garden - suggests heedlessness and transgression: 犯. Through miscarriage of justice, many an offender gets away with transgression; so laments the proverb: "The black dog eats the meat; the white dog is punished."

丿	犭	犭	狛	犯
1	2	3	4	5

狼 **hěn**
fierce; vicious; cruel

狼毒	hěn dú	vicious
狠心	hěn xīn	heartless
凶狠	xiōng hěn	ferocious and ruthless

艮, the phonetic, is the classical abbreviation of 𥃩, made up of 目 (eye) and 匕 (turn). It signifies to turn around and look a man defiantly in the face. With the addition of the dog radical(犭), indicating beastliness, it means: fierce, vicious, cruel or quarrelsome. But, concludes the proverb: "A good dog does not fight with chickens, nor a good man with his wife."

ノ	犭	犭	犭	犭	犭	犭	狠	狠
1	2	3	4	5	6	7	8	9

狼 **láng**
wolf

狼狗	láng gǒu	wolfhound
狼獾	láng huān	glutton
狼籍	láng jí	scattered about in a mess
豺狼	chái láng	jackal

The wolf: 狼 has dog (犭) for radical. The phonetic: 艮 was originally 㫔, modified to 昆 signifies a gift(曰) - godly nature, coming down from above(尸). 㫖, the modification, shows heaven and earth coming together (廾) with the gift (曰) eventually becoming lost (厶). 狼 therefore suggests wolf - a dog that has lost its virtuous nature and acquired a vicious one. Hence the proverbial warning: "Outside he is clothed in a sheep's skin; inside his heart is a wolf's."

ノ	犭	犭	犭	犭	犭	犭	狼	狼	狼
1	2	3	4	5	6	7	8	9	10

狮 **shī**
lion

狮子	shī zi	lion
狮子狗	shī zǐ gǒu	pug-dog
狮子舞	shī zǐ wǔ	lion dance
狮子座	shī zǐ zuò	leo (of the horoscope)

The radical is the character for dog or beast (犭). The phonetic: 師 signifies the first (一) banner(巾)over the fort (𠂤), i.e., the banner of the commander-in-chief, and means: leader or master. Clarified by the dog radical (犭). the idea is set forth that the king or master (師) of beasts (犭) is the lion: 狮.

ノ	犭	犭	狮	狮	狮	狮	狮	狮
1	2	3	4	5	6	7	8	9

猫 māo
cat

小猫	xiǎo māo	kitten
雄猫	xióng māo	tom cat
熊猫	xióng māo	panda

The radical:犭is a pictograph depicting a feline, a cat with its head, whiskers, paws and backbone. The older form:貓 juxtaposes cat (犭)and sprout (苗) to denote that cats eat mice - destroyers of grain sprouts (艹) in the field (田). The enmity between cats and dogs is emphasised in the proverb: "if the dog goes when the cat comes, there will be no fight." However, in the modern form: 猫 , the cat (犭) goes when the dog (犭)comes."

ノ	犭	犭	犭	犷	犷	犷	猫	猫	猫	猫			
1	2	3	4	5	6	7	8	9	10	11			

马 mǎ
horse

马鞍	mǎ ān	saddle
马鞭	mǎ biān	horsewhip
马车	mǎ chē	horse-drawn carriage
马虎	mǎ hū	careless; casual
马上	mǎ shàng	at once; immediately

馬 is a picturesque representation of a brawny horse rearing. It has since undergone drastic changes, losing eyes and mane. The simplified form reduces it to three masterly strokes: 马 - a skeleton horse, advanced in age but rich in experience, inspiring the proverb: "The old horse knows the way."

乛	马	马											
1	2	3											

骡 luó
mule

骡夫	luó fū	a muleteer
骡马	luó mǎ	mules and horses
骡子	luó zi	mule (the off-spring of an ass and a mare)

The phonetic 累 gives a clue to the identity of this member of the horse (馬) family. 累 was originally(纍), three article (畾)connected or tied (糸) together, and means involved or accumulated, troublesome or unmanageable, burdened or tired. These traits characterise the mule: 骡 , a beast of burden, noted for being stubborn. Its sluggishness prompts the saying: "A person riding a mule does not realise the slowness of walking."

乛	马	马	马	马	马	骡	骡	骡	骡	骡	骡	骡	骡
1	2	3	4	5	6	7	8	9	10	11	12	13	14

骆 luò
camel

骆驼	luò tuó	camel
骆驼队	luò tuó duì	camel train; caravan
骆驼绒	luò tuó róng	camel's hair material

馬 , representing a horse or beast of burden, is the radical. 各 , the phonetic, means to go one's way unconcernedly, without heeding others. This dominant characteristic of the self-sufficient camel: 骆 ,an animal blessed with great endurance and ability to go without food and water for weeks.

㇇	马	马	马'	驴	驭	驭	骆	骆			
1	2	3	4	5	6	7	8	9			

尘 chén
dust; dirt

尘埃	chén āi	dust
尘暴	chén bào	dust storm
尘肺	chén fèi	pneumoconiosis
尘垢	chén gòu	dust and dirt
尘土	chén tǔ	dust
尘污	chén wū	soiled with dust
尘嚣	chén xiāo	hubbub; uproar

The original form showed three deer (鹿) running over the earth (土), stirring up a trail of dust (塵). The regular form reduced the number of deer to one. The simplified form breaks it down further to tiny (⼩) particles of earth (土), forming dust or dirt: (尘) .

⼁	⼩	小	少	尘'	尘						
1	2	3	4	5	6						

庆 qìng
celebrate; congratulate

庆典	qìng diǎn	celebration
庆贺	qìng hè	celebrate
庆幸	qìng xìng	rejoice
庆祝	qìng zhù	celebrate

In ancient times it was traditional to go (夂) and offer, on a festive day, a deer's (鹿) skin with hearty (心) wishes. Hence: 慶 , to celebrate, congratulate or bring a blessing. The simplified form for celebration puts it in a nutshell: something big (大) under cover or roof (广) - a big occasion indoors.

、	亠	广	广'	庄	庆						
1	2	3	4	5	6						

丽 lì

beautiful;
handsome;
elegant

| 丽人 | lì rén | a beauty |
| 美丽 | měi lì | beautiful |

This character for beauty and elegance is a picture of the graceful deer (鹿) decorated with a pair of pendants (丽). The simplified form displays the pair of pendants linked together: 丽. Physical attractiveness is not to be envied, if we go by the saying: "Beautiful women generally suffer an evil fate; intelligent young men are seldom handsome."

| 一 | 丆 | 丂 | 帀 | 兩 | 丽 | 丽 | | |
| 1 | 2 | 3 | 4 | 5 | 6 | 7 | | |

虎 hǔ

tiger

虎伏	hǔ fú	gyro wheel
虎将	hǔ jiàng	brave general
虎劲	hǔ jìn	dauntless drive; dash
虎钳	hǔ qián	vice
虎穴	hǔ xué	tiger's den
老虎	lǎo hǔ	tiger

The character for tiger is a pictograph. It is based on the radical cal 虍 (tiger skin) clarified by 几 (hind legs): 虎. Characterised by its vicious ferocity, the tiger strikes fear even when dead. Hence the saying: "He who rides the tiger finds it difficult to dismount." (骑虎难下)

| 丨 | 上 | 斥 | 虍 | 卢 | 虍 | 虎 | 虎 | |
| 1 | 2 | 3 | 4 | 5 | 6 | 7 | 8 | |

号 háo or hào

shout
mark;
number

号哭	háo kū	wail
号叫	háo jiào	howl; yet
号称	hào chēng	known as; claim to be
号令	hào lìn	order
号码	hào mǎ	number
号召	hào zhào	call; appeal

号 comes from mouth (口) uttering an exclamation (, the breathrising against an obstacle 一). 号 therefore means to cry out. The presence of the tiger (虎) gives the needed impetus to shout: 號. In the simplified form, the tiger is eliminated: 号. 號 also means mark or number, usually announced by the mouth, with a call or cry.

| 丶 | 口 | 口 | 므 | 号 | | | | |
| 1 | 2 | 3 | 4 | 5 | | | | |

象

xiàng
elephant

象鼻	xiàng bí	trunk (of an elephant)
象棋	xiàng qí	Chinese chess
象散	xiàng sàn	astigmatism
象限	xiàng xiàn	quadrant
象牙	xiàng yá	elephant's tusk; ivory
象样	xiàng yàng	presentable

This character is a striking image of the elephant, emphasising its trunk and precious tusks: 象. Valuable possessions can pose a hazard to life; in the words of the proverb: "The elephant is killed because of its tusks."

ノ	⺈	⺈	刍	刍	尹	争	多	多	象	象						
1	2	3	4	5	6	7	8	9	10	11						

像

xiàng
portrait; image

像样	xiàng yàng	up to the mark; presentable; decent
像话	xiàng huà	reasonable; proper; right
人像	rén xiàng	portrait; image

In this character the phonetic 象 means elephant and also image. The radical 亻 (man) clarifies its application to man and means image, portrait or resemblance: 像 Man has been making images of everything imaginable under and above the sun. So, reasons the proverb: "No image-maker worships the gods; he knows what they are made of."

ノ	イ	イ	伫	伫	侉	侉	俜	侉	像	像	像	像				
1	2	3	4	5	6	7	8	9	10	11	12	13				

熊

xióng
bear

熊蜂	xióng fēng	bumble bee
熊猴	xióng hóu	Assamese macaque
熊猫	xióng māo	panda
狗熊	gǒu xióng	Asiatic black bear

能 is a representation of the bear, with its head (厶), hairy body (月) and paws (匕). The bear is a symbol of bravery, and is extremely strong and able. Hence: 能 , meaning able. To differentiate bear from ability (能) four dots (灬) standing for feet are added: 熊 .

厶	厶	疒	台	台	肖	肖	能	能	能	能	能	熊	熊			
1	2	3	4	5	6	7	8	9	10	11	12	13	14			

tù
hare; rabbit

兔狲	tù sūn	steppe cat
兔脱	tù tuō	run away like a hare; escape; flee
兔子	tù zi	rabbit; hare
白兔	bái tù	white rabbit

兔 Is a pitograph of the squatting hare or rabbit, with its tall perked up. Noted for its shrewdness In the struggle for survival, the proverbial hare has three holes to its burrow - and it does not eat the grass around it.

丿	𠂆	𠂇	厶	臼	尹	兔	兔					
1	2	3	4	5	6	7	8					

---

yuān
oppression; injustice

冤仇	yuān chóu	enmity
冤家	yuān jiā	foe; enemy
冤屈	yuān qū	wrongful treatment
冤头	yuān tóu	enemy; foe
冤柱	yuān wang	treat unjustly

An inoffensive hare (兔) confined under a cover (冖) suggests oppression: 冤. By extension, 冤 also means injustice and false accusation. Oppression has long established Itself In human society but, asserts the proverb: "A house established by oppression cannot long enjoy prosperity."

丶	冖	冖	冖	冖	冤	冤	冤	冤	冤		
1	2	3	4	5	6	7	8	9	10		

---

yì
escape; leisure

逸乐	yì lè	comfort and pleasure
逸民	yì mín	hermit (in ancient times); recluse
逸闻	yì wén	ancsdote
逃逸	táo yì	escape

The radical 乚 means to go fast and stop suddenly. Combined with 兔 (rabbit), it suggests a rabbit on the run, and means to flee, escape or retire from the world. The hare, being regarded as a profligate, 逸 also means to lead an idle and licentious life.

丿	𠂆	𠂇	厶	臼	尹	兔	兔	逸	逸	逸	
1	2	3	4	5	6	7	8	9	10	11	

鼠 shǔ
rat; mouse

鼠辈	shǔ bèi	scoundrels
鼠疫	shǔ yì	plague
老鼠	lǎo shǔ	mouse; rat

鼠 refers to rodents in general - from the timid mouse to the aggressive rat. It is a pictograph of the rat, showing its head, whiskers and tail: 鼠. A young rat may know how to gnaw its hole but, warns the proverb: "A rat that gnaws at a cat's tail invites destruction."

丶	亻	冂	冃	臼	白	臼	臼	鼡	鼡	鼡	鼡	鼠
1	2	3	4	5	6	7	8	9	10	11	12	13

窜 cuàn
hide; flee

窜犯	cuàn fàn	raid; make an inroad into
窜改	cuàn gǎi	tamper with; alter
窜扰	cuàn rǎo	harass
窜逃	cuàn táo	flee in disorder
鼠窜	shǔ cuàn	scurry like rats

穴 is a hole obtained by removing or separating (八)rock or earth. A mouse(鼠) in its hole(穴) produces竄, meaning to hide, flee or escape. The simplified form substitutes串 for鼠 to form窜.串 is an ideo graph suggesting two objects (吕) strung together 串, and means to string, pierce or bore. Hence窜 to escape by boring (串) a hole (穴).

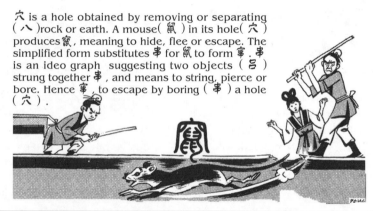

丶	宀	宀	宀	穴	穴	窏	窏	窏	窜	窜	窜
1	2	3	4	5	6	7	8	9	10	11	12

集 jí
assemble; gather together

集合	jí hé	gather
集会	jí huì	assembly
集锦	jí jǐn	a collection of choice specimens
集市	jí shì	country fair; market
集体	jí tǐ	collective

The ancient character depicted three birds (雥) flocking together atop a tree (木). This was eventually contracted to 集: bird (隹) on tree (木). A gathering of birds may have created the character for "assembly" but, as the saying goes: "A gathering of mosquitoes can create a noise like thunder."

丿	亻	亻	亻	乍	乍	隹	隹	隹	隹	集	集
1	2	3	4	5	6	7	8	9	10	11	12

只 zhī
one; single

只身　zhī shēn　　alone; by oneself
一只　yī zhī　　used as a numerative or classifier

A bird (隹) in hand (又) means "one" or "single": 隻 and is used as a numerative or classifier for birds, animals, ships and single individuals of things in pairs or sets, as arm, eye, hand, shoe, etc. It is now replaced by the simplified form: 只 , which, incidentally, means "only."

`	口	口	尸	只												
1	2	3	4	5												

双 shuāng
a pair

双边　shuāng biān　bilateral
双层　shuāng céng　two layers
双重　shuāng chóng　double
双方　shuāng fāng　both sides
双亲　shuāng qīn　(both) parents
双生　shuāng shēng　twin
双喜　shuāng xǐ　double happiness

Just as one bird (隹) in hand (又) means single: 隻, so two birds (隹隹) in hand (又) stand for a pair: 雙 . The simplified form shows just two hands: 双 - a clearer representation because hands, unlike birds, always come in pairs. Unfortunately, according to the saying, "Blessings never come in pairs, nor misfortunes singly."

フ	又	双	双													
1	2	3	4													

进 jìn
advance; enter

进步　jìn bù　　progress; advance
进度　jìn dù　　rate of progress
进攻　jìn gōng　attack
进化　jìn huà　　evolution
进食　jìn shí　　have one's meal
进行　jìn xíng　　be in progress
进展　jìn zhǎn　make progress

This character is made up of "move" (辶,contraction of 辵) and "bird"(隹). When birds "move" they always fly forward, never backward. So 進 means to "advance." In the simplified form, 井 (order) replaces(bird), suggesting advancement and, by extension, entry: 进 - an orderly movement encouraged by the proverb: "He who does not advance loses ground" (不进则退) .

一	二	于	井	汫	讲	进										
1	2	3	4	5	6	7										

售 shòu
sell

售货	shòu huò	sell goods
售价	shòu jià	selling price
售卖	shòu mài	sell
出售	chū shòu	offer for sale
售票员	shòu piào yuán	ticket seller; conductor

The original ideograph for "sell" represented two birds (雔) the buyer and the seller, haggling with the mouth (口). The modern character shows only one bird (隹), the seller, marketing his wares with the mouth (口). The proverb explains the absence of the buyer: "Fuel is not sold in the forest, nor fish on the shore of the lake."

ノ	イ	イ	乍	乍	乍	隹	隹	隹	隹	售										
1	2	3	4	5	6	7	8	9	10	11										

焦 jiāo
burnt; scorched

焦点	jiāo diǎn	focal point
焦化	jiāo huà	coking
焦黄	jiāo huáng	sallow; brown
焦急	jiāo jí	anxious
焦距	jiāo jù	focal distance; focal length
焦虑	jiāo lǜ	feel anxious

Bird (隹) over fire (灬) means "burnt or scorched": 焦, and by extension, "worried or anxious." Man has always felt like a bird over fire. In the words of the saying: "One does not live a hundred years, yet worries enough for a thousand."

ノ	イ	イ	乍	乍	乍	隹	隹	隹	隹	焦	焦									
1	2	3	4	5	6	7	8	9	10	11	12									

离 lí
part; leave; separate

离别	lí bié	part; bid farewell
离婚	lí hūn	divorce
离间	lí jiàn	sow discord
离境	lí jìng	leave a country or place
离奇	lí qí	odd; fantastic
距离	jù lí	distance

離 was formerly used for the oriole, an elegant golden bird - 离 meaning uncanny and 隹 meaning bird. When the oriole made its rare appearance in spring, it was the signal for daughters of marriageable age to wed and leave their parental home; hence the idea of "to leave." 隹 has since separated from 离, leaving the simplified form: 离

丶	亠	宀	文	䒑	卤	卤	离	离	离											
1	2	3	4	5	6	7	8	9	10											

鸡 jī
chicken

鸡蛋	jī dàn	chicken's egg
鸡毛	jī máo	chicken's feather
鸡肉	jī ròu	meat of chicken
公鸡	gōng jī	cock; rooster
母鸡	mǔ jī	hen
鸡蛋糕	jī dàn gāo	sponge cake

The radical 鸟 stands for bird. The phonetic 奚 signifies an adult (大) with hand (爪 or) on silk thread (纟 or 幺) - a spinner. Previously women prisoners were condemned to spinning without getting any benefit, not unlike the chicken confined to the labour of laying eggs for its owner. A bird (鸟) in hand (又) produces the simplified chicken: 鸡 , a really handy bird.

丁	又	又′	又丁	劝	鸡	鸡								
1	2	3	4	5	6	7								

鸭 yā
duck

鸭蛋	yā dàn	duck's egg
鸭绒	yā róng	duck's down; elderdown
公鸭	gōng yā	drake
母鸭	mǔ yā	duck
小鸭	xiǎo yā	duckling
鸭舌帽	yā shé mào	peaked cap

甲 - meaning armour, protective covering or shell - is the distinguishing phonetic here. The duck is probably the hardiest of birds, with a natural immunity to disease and ability to withstand severe envornmental conditions. Hence: 鸭 , the well-protected (甲) bird (鸟). Nevertheless, the proverb has the last word: "Compare a duck with a goose, and the duck will be unsaleable."

丨	冂	日	日	甲	甲′	甲丁	甲丁	鸭	鸭					
1	2	3	4	5	6	7	8	9	10					

鸽 gē
dove; pigeon

鸽子	gē zi	pigeon; dove
家鸽	jiā gē	domestic pigeon
野鸽	yě gē	wild pigeon
鸽子笼	gē zi lóng	pigeon cote

合 indicates harmony of many 厶 mouths (口), 厶 symbolising unity and agreement of three lines forming a balanced triangle. 鸽 ideographically refers to the dove or pigeon - the bird (鸟) that flocks together in peace, harmony and unity (合).

丿	人	𠂉	𠆢	合	合	合′	合丁	合丁	鸽	鸽				
1	2	3	4	5	6	7	8	9	10	11				

凤

fèng
phoenix (male)

凤凰	fèng huáng	phoenix
凤梨	fèng lí	pineapple
凤尾鱼	fèng wěi yú	anchovy

Originally, the phoenix was represented by 絊 (朋), its tail. As it flew, it drew all birds to it in friendship. Eventually became a symbol of friendship, and a new character was adopted for the phoenix: 鳳 - a pictograph of the bird - relating it to wind (風) in sound and symbol. The simplified form substitutes a friendly hand (又) for the friendly phoenix: 凤.

ノ	几	凡	凤												
1	2	3	4												

燕

yàn
swallow

燕麦	yàn mài	oats
燕鸥	yàn ōu	tern
燕隼	yàn sǔn	hobby
燕窝	yàn wō	edible bird's nest
燕鱼	yàn yú	Spanish mackerel
燕子	yàn zi	swallow
燕尾服	yàn wěi fú	tuxedo

燕 is a symmetrical pictograph of the swallow flying upwards. Swallows abound in the northern hemisphere and are always a welcome sight in spring. The swallow (燕) is fondly remembered as a bird from the north (北), flying across the waters (灬) with a stalk (一) of grass (廿) in its mouth (口).

一	十	廿	廿	艹	苎	苎	苩	苗	苗	莁	燕	燕	燕	燕	燕
1	2	3	4	5	6	7	8	9	10	11	12	13	14	15	16

不

bù
not

不安	bù ān	uneasy; disturbed
不便	bù biàn	inconvenient
不断	bù duàn	continuous
不顾	bù gù	in spite of; regardless of
不客气	bù kè qi	impolite

This character represents a bird flying up towards the sky and disappearing from sight, as if becoming non-existent. The horizontal stroke (一) signifies the sky as the limit, blocking the bird (小) from ever reaching its destination. Hence the idea of "net", a negative: 不. Arrogant man, unable even to walk with his fellowman, now tries to fly; to him also, the sky is the limit.

一	丆	不	不												
1	2	3	4												

歪 wāi
crooked

歪风	wāi fēng	unhealthy trend
歪曲	wāi qū	distort; misrepresent
歪诗	wāi shī	inelegant verses; doggerel
歪斜	wāi xié	crooked

歪 Is an ideograph composed of two characters: 不 (not) and 正 (upright). It means: not straight, i.e., crooked. 正 itself indicates stopping(止) at a line or limit (一), without going astray, hence upright. Although imperfect, we do well to heed the proverbial counsel: "Stand upright, and don't worry If your shadow is crooked."

一	ナ	才	不	丕	歪	歪	歪	歪
1	2	3	4	5	6	7	8	9

至 zhì
arrive; reach

至诚	zhì chéng	utmost sincerity
至多	zhì duō	at the most
至交	zhì jiāo	most intimate friend
至今	zhì jīn	up to now; so far
至上	zhì shàng	supreme; the highest

The character 至 is the opposite of 不 which represents a bird flying straight upwards but unable to reach its destination. The original form (坐) is a pictograph of a bird, bending its wings and darting downwards to the earth and reaching it. 至 is the modern form, meaning: arrive or reach.

一	工	云	丞	至	至
1	2	3	4	5	6

屋 wū
house

屋顶	wū dǐng	roof
屋脊	wū jǐ	ridge (of a roof)
屋架	wū jià	roof truss
屋檐	wū yán	eaves
屋宇	wū yǔ	house
屋子	wū zi	dwelling place

The phonetic 至 means to arrive or reach, and the radical 尸 is a reclining figure. 屋 is where you recline(尸)on arrival(至)- a place of rest, a house. And a house, once built, is permanently at rest; hence the saying: "Before you build a house, know your neighbourhood."

一	冖	尸	尸	序	层	屋	屋	屋
1	2	3	4	5	6	7	8	9

室 shì
room; chamber

室外	shì wài	outdoor
课室	kè shì	classroom
卧室	wò shì	bedroom
会客室	huì kè shì	reception room
办公室	bàn gōng shì	office

The ideograph 室 suggests arrival (至)at a destination under a roof (宀), i.e., a room enclosed by walls. And because there are two sides to the wall, "One family builds a wall, two families enjoy it."

`、 丷 宀 宀 宀 宊 宊 宊 室`
1 2 3 4 5 6 7 8 9

龟 gui
tortoise

龟板	guī bǎn	tortoise plastron
龟背	guī bèi	curvature of the spinal column
龟甲	guī jiǎ	tortoise-shell
龟缩	guī suō	withdraw into passive defence
乌龟	wū guī	tortoise

The tortoise is a symbol of longevity, having a life span of over 150 years. Unreasoning and coldblooded but harmless, it is described as an animal with its "flesh inside and bones outside." The character for tortoise is a pictograph, with an evolutionary history as slow and steady as the creature itself.

`丿 ⺈ ⺈ 乌 乌 白 龟`
1 2 3 4 5 6 7

万 wàn
myriad; 10,000

万般	wàn bān	all the different kinds
万端	wàn duān	multifarious
万分	wàn fēn	very much; extremely
万古	wàn gǔ	eternally; forever
万能	wàn néng	omnipotent

A pictograph of the scorpion: 萬 was used for 10,000 or myriad by sound loan. When it came to simplification, the Indian swastika: 卐 (meaning also 10,000) was borrowed and stylised to 万 . The term 万岁 (10,000 years) became the title of the emperor, despite the saying: "the emperor has money but he cannot buy myriads of years to live."

`一 丆 万`
1 2 3

易 yì
change; easy

易经	Yì Jīng	The Book of Changes
轻易	qīng yì	easily
容易	róng yì	easy
易燃物	yì rán wù	combustibles; inflammables

易 bears the likeness of a chameleon, a lizard that changes its colour easily to blend with its background. This change of colour is "as easy as turning over one's palm" (易如反掌). Hence the extended meaning: change or easy.

| ㇐ | 冂 | 曰 | 日 | 月 | 弓 | 昜 | 易 | | | | | | | | | | |
| 1 | 2 | 3 | 4 | 5 | 6 | 7 | 8 | | | | | | | | | | |

龙 lóng
dragon

龙船	lóng chuán	dragon boat
龙卷	lóng juǎn	spout
龙虾	lóng xiā	lobster
龙眼	lóng yǎn	longan
龙钟	lóng zhōng	senile
龙卷风	lóng juǎn fēng	tornado

The primitive form was a pictograph of the dragon:🐉. The regular form: 龙, although resembling the royal creature, is made up of(contraction of 飞, wings), 月 (body). and 立 (contraction of the phonetic 童, slave boy). 龙 also means imperial or glorious; hence the saying: "With money you are a dragon, without it you are a worm."

| 一 | 𠂇 | 九 | 龙 | 龙 | | | | | | | | | | | | | |
| 1 | 2 | 3 | 4 | 5 | | | | | | | | | | | | | |

角 jiǎo
horn; corner; 10-cent piece

角尺	jiǎo chǐ	angle square
角度	jiǎo dù	angle
角落	jiǎo luò	corner; nook
角膜	jiǎo mó	cornea
角质	jiǎo zhì	cutin
号角	hào jiǎo	bugle
鹿角	lù jiǎo	antler

The radical 角 resembles a horn with its streaks. It is probably a combination of 力 (strong) and 月 (flesh). Because the horn terminates in an angle and tapers to a point, 角 can mean angle or corner. 角 is also a 10-cent piece, a mere tenth or "corner" of a dollar.

| ノ | 勹 | 𠂊 | 角 | 角 | 角 | 角 | | | | | | | | | | | |
| 1 | 2 | 3 | 4 | 5 | 6 | 7 | | | | | | | | | | | |

解 jiě
divide;
untie;
explain

解除	jiě chú	remove
解答	jiě dǎ	answer; explain
解雇	jiě gù	discharge; dismiss
解决	jiě jué	solve; dispose of
解开	jiě kāi	untie
解闷	jiě mèn	divert oneself from boredom
解剖	jiě pōu	dissect

This character combines the radical for horn（角）with knife（刀）and ox（牛）. To cleave the horn of an ox requires the use of a knife; hence 解: to divide. The horn of an ox is also shaped into bodkins（刀）for untying knots. So 解 also means to untie, undo, unravel and, by extension, explain. The ancient lexicon 说文解字 explains the origin of Chinese characters.

ノ	ケ	ク	角	角	角	角	角	解	解	解	解	解
1	2	3	4	5	6	7	8	9	10	11	12	13

毛 máo
hair; fur;
10-cent
piece

毛笔	máo bǐ	writing brush
毛纺	máo fǎng	wool spinning
毛巾	máo jīn	towel
毛孔	máo kǒng	pore
毛毯	máo tǎn	wollen blanket
毛线	máo xiàn	knitting wool
毛衣	máo yī	wollen sweater

毛 is a pictograph of the hair of man or beast. Compared with other parts of the body, the hair is insignificant and valueless. 毛 also means little, unpolished, or the common 10- cent piece. Our hairs may not be numbered but, says the proverb: "pull a hair and the whole body may be affected."

ノ	二	三	毛
1	2	3	4

尾 wěi
tail; end

尾巴	wěi bā	tail
尾灯	wěi dēng	tail light; tail lamp
尾欠	wěi qiàn	balance due
尾声	wěi shēng	epilogue; end
尾随	wěi suí	tag along; follow at somebody's heel
尾追	wěi zhuī	in hot pursuit

尾 has 尸 (a recumbent body) as radical and 毛 (hair) as phonetic. In the seal form 毛 is inverted, Indicating hair growing downwards from the body（尸）, suggesting a tail:. The tail is meant to be wagged by the body but when the people are strong and the ruler weak, "The tail is too large to wag"（尾大不掉）.

ㄱ	尸	尸	尸	尼	尾	尾
1	2	3	4	5	6	7

老 lǎo
old; aged

老板	lǎo bǎn	boss; employer
老成	lǎo chéng	experienced; steady
老将	lǎo jiàng	veteran; old-timer
老练	lǎo liàn	seasoned; experienced
老年	lǎo nián	old age
老实	lǎo shí	honest; frank

The seal character for "old" grew out of 毛 (hair), 人 (person) and 匕 (change). When the hair of man turns gray or white, its colour has changed, indicating old age: 耂, now arbitrarily shrunk to 老. To encourage respect for white hair, the old saying warns: "Laugh at the old, and age will laugh at you."

一 十 土 耂 耂 老
1 2 3 4 5 6

票 piào
bill; ticket; ballot

票额	piào é	the sum stated on a cheque or bill; denomination
票房	piào fáng	booking office
票根	piào gēn	counterfoil; stub
票价	piào jià	the price of a ticket

The early seal form: represents an ancient method of signalling fire (火) with rising smoke (彡) manipulated by four hands (臼). This suggests ticket or ballot form of sign. Another seal form: depicts the mischievous fairy of the phantom-fire, a dreaded natural phenomenon. It stands for bill or warrant - things also dreaded. The modern arbitrary form: 票 may be remembered as a bank bill, a western (西) token (示).

一 ⺊ 二 币 西 西 覀 覀 票 票 票
1 2 3 4 5 6 7 8 9 10 11

爬 pá
crawl; creep; climb

爬 combines two pictographs: 爪 and 巴. 爪 (claw) is the right hand, palm down, resting on the finger-tips; 巴 (boa) is a snake raised on its tail. Hence 爬: to crawl, creep or climb, like a snake. Climbing is not plain sailing according to the saying: "Following virtue is like climbing a hill; following vice is like sailing downstream."

爬虫	pá chóng	reptile; insect
爬竿	pá gān	climbing pole; pole-climbing
爬犁	pá lí	sledge
爬山	pá shān	mountain-climbing
爬行	pá xíng	crawl; creep

丿 厂 爪 爪 爬 爬 爬 爬
1 2 3 4 5 6 7 8

为　wèi or wéi

because;
to be;
to do

为何	wèi hé	why
为难	wéi nán	feel awkward; make things difficult
为期	wéi qī	by a definite date; duration
为人	wéi rén	behave; conduct oneself

A pictograph based on reason, 爲 originally was a female monkey with a human body: 鸞 because of the resemblance. It was borrowed for because" and 'contracted to two claws: 爭 because the female monkey was most prone to claw. To include the meaning "to do, to be" it took on a more human form: 爲, a hand carding textile fibres to remove unessntials, leading to the simplified form: 为

丶	ﾉ	为	为
1	2	3	4

争　zhēng

contend;
fight;
quarrel

争辩	zhēng biàn	argue
争吵	zhēng chǎo	quarrel
争持	zhēng chí	refuse to give in
争斗	zhēng dòu	fight; struggle; strife
争夺	zhēng duó	fight
争论	zhēng lùn	controversy;

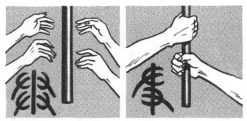

This ideograph features two hands tugging at an object. The older forms graphically portray the quarrel or fight between two pairs of hands. Though the left hand conquers the right, no advantage is gained. Hence: "pottery and fine porcelain must not fight" and "Eggs must not quarrel with stones."

ﾉ	⺈	⺈	乌	刍	争		
1	2	3	4	5	6		

受　shòu

receive;
accept

受苦	shòu kǔ	suffer
受难	shòu nàn	suffer calamities
受罚	shòu fá	be punished
受害	shòu hài	victimised
受气	shòu qì	be bullied
受伤	shòu shāng	be wounded
受益	shòu yì	benefit from

This character represents the loading of goods. A hand (爪), on the bank, delivers the goods while another hand(又), in the boat, (舟) receives and stows them away in the hold. In the seal forms the boat can be seen in symbol: 夕, eventually contracted to 冖 and ⌒. The ideograph, by extension, means "receive, accept, endure."

⺈	⺈	⺈	⺈	⺤	受	受	受
1	2	3	4	5	6	7	8

骨 gǔ
bone

骨骼	gǔ gé	skeleton
骨灰	gǔ huī	ashes of the dead
骨架	gǔ jià	framework
骨节	gǔ jié	joint
骨牌	gǔ pái	dominoes
骨气	gǔ qì	moral integrity
骨肉	gǔ ròu	flesh and blood

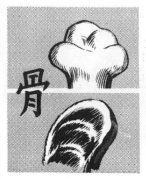

The bones form the framework of the body and are closely associated with the flesh. The character for bone: 骨 therefore combines pictographs of the bone 冎 and flesh (肉). However, courtesy demands that you ask for a bone if you want flesh, despite the saying: "You can't get fat from a dry bone."

⼁	冂	冋	冎	冎	骨	骨	骨	骨						
1	2	3	4	5	6	7	8	9						

皮 pí
skin;
leather

皮袄	pí ǎo	fur-lined jacket
皮包	pí bāo	leather handbag
皮带	pí dài	leather belt
皮蛋	pí dàn	preserved egg
皮肤	pí fū	skin
皮箱	pí xiāng	leather suitcase
皮鞋	pí xié	leather shoes

Three compenents make up the character for skin: 又, the hand that flays; 丿, the animal skin; and 刀, the knife. The animal skin, being durable, may be compared to the reputation of a man, as in the saying: "man dies and leaves a name; the tiger dies and leaves a skin."

一	厂	广	皮	皮										
1	2	3	4	5										

风 fēng
wind

风采	fēng cǎi	elegant demeanour
风干	fēng gān	air-dry
风格	fēng gé	style
风光	fēng guāng	scene; view
风浪	fēng làng	stormy waves; storm
风靡	fēng mǐ	fashionable

The seal form: 鳳 is based on man's belief that insects(虫) are born under the influence of the wind or vapour (凡). An older form: 颪 - from 日 (sun), 丿 (motion) and 几 (extension) - suggests that wind is produced by the action of the sun. The simplified form, however, cuts out the sun and insects, leaving the moti on and extension; 风, which goes to prove that "man's words are like grass - they sway with the wind."

丿	几	凤	风											
1	2	3	4											

公 **gōng**
public;
impartial

公道	gōng dào	reasonable
公共	gōng gòng	public
公分	gōng fēn	centimetre (cm)
公民	gōng mín	citizen
公式	gōng shì	formula
公司	gōng sī	company; corporation
公用	gōng yòng	for public use

A is made up of 丨八 (division, opposition) and ㄙ (private, selfish), a pictograph of a silkworm coiled in its cocoon. It implies the division (八) of private (ㄙ) property for the benefit of the public. Hence 公, meaning public or impartial, i.e., opposed (八) to private or selfish (ㄙ).

ノ 八 公 公
1 2 3 4

私 **sī**
personal;
private;
selfish

私奔	sī bēn	elopement
私立	sī lì	privately run
私人	sī rén	private
私事	sī shì	private (or personal) affairs
私语	sī yǔ	whisper
无私	wú sī	selfless

The radical 禾 stands for grain, man's staple food, a highly valued possession. The phonetic ㄙ, representing a silkworm hidden in its cocoon, symbolises private or selfish. Grain (禾) in ancient days was used to pay taxes and the residue was personal (ㄙ) property. Hence 私: my share of grain, i.e., personal, private or selfish.

一 二 千 禾 禾 私 私
1 2 3 4 5 6 7

丝 **sī**
silk

丝绸	sī chóu	silk cloth
丝带	sī dài	silk ribbon; silk braid; silk sash
丝毫	sī háo	a bit
丝绒	sī róng	velvet
丝状	sī zhuàng	filiform
肉丝	ròu sī	meat floss

糸 is the seal form of 糸, the radical for silk. The upper 8 represents two cocoons; the lower part ㅅ, the twisting of several strands into a thread. 糸 is duplicated to stand for silk, indicating that many threads are required to form silk: 絲. In the modern version the two Identical components are woven together and simplified to 丝.

乙 幺 丝 丝 丝
1 2 3 4 5

线 xiàn
thread

线虫	xiàn chóng	nematode
线段	xiàn duàn	line segment
线描	xiàn miáo	line drawing
线绳	xiàn shéng	cotton rope
线索	xiàn suǒ	clue
光线	guāng xiàn	traditional thread binding (of Chinese books)

The radical is 糸 (silk). The phonetic 戔 means small, fine or split into bits - the common work of many spears (戈). Hence 缐 : thread, made up of minute (戔) strands of silk (糸) . Another version is 綫 , with 泉 (spring) as phonetic. Here the thread is likened to a continuous flow of water from a spring. Whichever the version, "The thread cannot pass without a needle: the boat cannot cross without water."

乄	乞	纟	纟	纟	线	线	线									
1	2	3	4	5	6	7	8									

红 hóng
red

红豆	hóng dòu	red beans; red seeds
红海	Hóng Hǎi	Red Sea
红利	hóng lì	bonus
红润	hóng rùn	rosy
红晕	hóng yùn	blush; flush
红运	hóng yùn	good luck

Red is a happy, auspicious colour, most pleasing to the Chinese. Because it is not the natural colour of slik (糸), extra work (工) has to be put in to dye it red: 红 . Red, however, is not always propitious, as in the saying: 红颜薄命 (Beautiful women are often unfortunate.)

乄	乞	纟	纟	红	红											
1	2	3	4	5	6											

给 gěi
give; provide; supply

给以	gěi yǐ	give; grant

Gifts foster unity and harmony (合) between friends and relatives; and what better present than silk (糸), a material appreciated by all. Hence 给 , meaning to give and, by extension, to provide or supply. The practice of giving brings blessings, for there is more happiness in giving than there is in receiving.

乄	乞	纟	纟	纵	纵	纶	给	给								
1	2	3	4	5	6	7	8	9								

结 jié

knot;
produce;
settle

结拜	jié bài	become sworn brothers or sisters
结冰	jié bīng	freeze
结彩	jié cǎi	adorn or decorate
结果	jié guǒ	result; outcome
结合	jié hé	combine
结婚	jié hūn	get married
结论	jié lùn	conclusion

The phonetic 吉 means fortunate - from 士 (affair) and 口 (mouth) - an affair worth announcing. In this character, the radical 纟 (silk) enforces the idea of tying or making secure something fortunate, e.g., concluding a contract, producing fruitage or tying a knot 结. Illustrated Is the successful conclusion of an affair worth announcing - the tying of the matrimonial knot.

纟	纟	纟	纟	纤	结	结	结	结
1	2	3	4	5	6	7	8	9

纸 zhǐ

paper

纸板	zhǐ bǎn	paperboard; cardboard
纸币	zhǐ bì	paper money; currency note
纸盒	zhǐ hé	box; carton
纸花	zhǐ huā	paper flower
纸牌	zhǐ pái	playing cards

The phonetic 氏 (clan) was originally a floating plant (屮)spread out flat (乇) over the water surface, rooting itself to the bottom. Silk (纟) - the radical - is also spread out when used as a writing material. Hence 纸 : paper - the writing material like silk (纟) that lies flat and apparently harmless as the water-plant(氏). But beware: "Paper and brush may kill a man; you don't need a knife."

纟	纟	纟	纟	红	纤	纸
1	2	3	4	5	6	7

网 wǎng

net

网罗	wǎng luó	trap
网球	wǎng qiú	tennis
电网	diàn wǎng	electrified barbed wire
发网	fà wǎng	hair net
鱼网	yú wǎng	fish net
蜘蛛网	zhī zhū wǎng	cobweb

This character started as a pictograph of a net: 网 . It was cast aside and replaced by the regular form 網, comprising 纟 (silk) and 岡 (trap) - without much success. So the primitive pictograph of the net was taken up again for the modern simplified form 网, demonstrating that "There is a day to cast your nets, and a day to dry your nets."

丨	冂	冂	网	网	网
1	2	3	4	5	6

细 xì

fine;
tender;
careful

细胞	xì bāo	cell
细长	xì cháng	tall and slender
细工	xì gōng	fine workmanship
细节	xì jié	minute detail
细菌	xì jūn	germ
细密	xì mì	fine and closely woven
细腻	xì nì	exquisite

In this character, the phonetic 田 was originally written: 囟, a top view of the child's skull showing the tender fontanelles. Hence 细, meaning tender, fine, soft, like the silken (纟) hair around the fontanelles (囟). Small beginnings are not to be despised for, just as resources last a long time if used sparingly, "A small stream flows without interruption."

乙	纟	纟	纠	纩	纫	细	细						
1	2	3	4	5	6	7	8						

经 jīng

classic;
already; pass
through

经常	jīng cháng	frequently
经典	jīng diǎn	classics
经度	jīng dù	longitude
经费	jīng fèi	funds
经管	jīng guǎn	be in charge of
经过	jīng guò	pass through; pass by

The phonetic 巠 was originally 巠- an allusion to water currents (巛) under the ground (一) that the geomancer examines (壬) something deep, not superficial In the regular form, the phonetic resembles warp threads on a loom: 巠. Just as silk threads (糸) are woven into precious fabrics, so wisdom is woven into enduring classics: 經 , a literary heritage that has already passed through many hands.

乙	纟	纟	纱	纭	经	纾	经						
1	2	3	4	5	6	7	8						

终 zhōng

end;
final

终点	zhōng diǎn	destination; finishing line
终古	zhōng gǔ	forever
终归	zhōng guī	eventually; after all
终究	zhōng jiū	eventually; in the end
终身	zhōng shēn	lifelong

This character has 冬 (winter) for its phonetic. Its seal form was a bundle of silk tied at the end by a band to suggest "end": 夅. Ice (冫) was added to signify winter, the end of the year. The presence of the silk radical (纟) extends the idea to "the winter of the silk thread" i.e., the final part of it, the end: 终 .

乙	纟	纟	纟	纱	终	终	终						
1	2	3	4	5	6	7	8						

yào
medicine

药草	yào cǎo	medicinal herbs
药方	yào fāng	prescription
药房	yào fáng	dispensary
药水	yào shuǐ	lotion; liquid medicine
药丸	yào wán	pill
服药	fú yào	take medicine
火药	huǒ yào	gunpowder

Medicinal herbs (艹), like music that soothes the mind, restore harmony (樂) to the body; hence 藥 the symbol for medicine. The simplified form 药 combines 艹 (herbs) with 约 (agree, restrain), implying that herbs restrain sickness. Though there are herbal remedies for all sorts of ailments: "No medicine can cure a man of vulgarity."

一	十	艹	艻	莎	药	药	药	药						
1	2	3	4	5	6	7	8	9						

xué
learn; study

学费	xué fèi	tuition fee
学府	xué fǔ	an institution of learning
学科	xué kē	branch of learning; subject
学生	xué shēng	student; pupil
学识	xué shí	knowledge

This ideograph signifies enlightenment - the master's laying on of hands (臼) crosswise 爻 upon the darkness which covers (冖) the mind of his disciple (子). It implies to learn or study. Learning is essential to the upbringing of a child, hence: "To raise a son without learning is raising an ass; to raise a daughter without learning is raising a pig."

丶	丷	丷	丷	丷	学	学	学							
1	2	3	4	5	6	7	8							

xiě
write

写实	xiě shí	write or paint realistically
写稿	xiě gǎo	write for (a magazine, etc.)
写生	xiě shēng	draw, paint or sketch from nature
写作	xiě zuò	writing

寫 originally was a picture of a magpie 舄 under a roof (宀). Regarded as a bird of good omen, the magpie is a tidy bird with the habit of picking up bright objects and hiding them 寫 therefore suggests order under the roof; by extension, to set one's ideas in order; to write, now simplified to 写 .

丶	冖	冖	写	写										
1	2	3	4	5										

印 yìn
print;
stamp;
seal

印发	yìn fā	print and distribute
印盒	yìn hé	seal box
印花	yìn huā	revenue stamp
印刷	yìn shuā	printing
印象	yìn xiàng	impression
印章	yìn zhāng	seal
盖印	gài yìn	affix one's seal

The right hand(⺕) pressing a seal(卩) formed the character for seals used for stamping impressions on clay: 印. These, in time, gave way to inked impressions on paper. With the invention of block printing and movable type, the character enlarged its meaning to include stamping and printing.

| ´ | ㇈ | 乍 | 印 | 印 | | | | |
| 1 | 2 | 3 | 4 | 5 | | | | |

书 shū
book;
writings

书包	shū bāo	schoolbag
书报	shū bào	books and newspapers
书本	shū běn	book
书店	shū diàn	bookshop
书法	shū fǎ	calligraphy
书房	shū fáng	study room

書 is the product of a pen (聿) that speaks (曰) books and writings. indicates a stylus(丨)in hand (ヨ) scratching a line (一) on a tablet(一). 曰, the radical, is the mouth (口) with a word (一) in it. Because not everything the pen speaks is truth, "It is better to have no books than to rely blindly on them."

| ㇇ | ㇈ | 书 | 书 | | | | | |
| 1 | 2 | 3 | 4 | | | | | |

画 huà
painting;
drawing

画报	huà bào	pictorial
画家	huà jiā	painter; artist
画架	huà jià	easel
画廊	huà láng	gallery
画室	huà shì	studio
画象	huà xiàng	portrait
画展	huà zhǎn	art exhibition

畫, a painting or drawing, is symbolised by the artist's brush (聿) and his picture (田); of the frame there now remains only the bottom part (一). However, the simplified form: 画 restores the picture(田) with its frame (凵). "Painting a snake and adding legs" (画蛇添足) would be superfluous. Hence the need to be practical: "you cannot satisfy your hunger by merely drawing a loaf."

| 一 | 厂 | 冂 | | | | |  |
| 1 | 2 | 3 | 4 | 5 | 6 | 7 | 8 |

王 wáng
king; ruler

国王	guó wáng	king
王朝	wáng cháo	imperial court; dynasty
王储	wáng chǔ	crown prince
王法	wáng fǎ	the law
王宫	wáng gōng	(imperial) palace
王牌	wáng pái	trump card
王室	wáng shì	royal family

Three horizontal planes (三) representing heaven, man and earth, connected by a vertical structure (丨), form the character for king: 王 - the one vested with power, between heaven and earth, to rule uprightly over man. Originally 王 was a pictograph of a string of jade beads (王) which only the royalty could afford. It eventually became the symbol for king.

一	二	千	王									
1	2	3	4									

玉 yù
jade; gem

玉雕	yù diāo	jade carving; jade sculpture
玉器	yù qì	jade article
玉色	yù sè	jade green; light bluish green
玉蜀黍	yù shǔ shǔ	maize; corn
玉簪	yù zān	jade hairpin

三 represents 3 pieces of jade strung together as a symbol for king: 王 The dot (丶) was added to form 玉 (jade), distinguishing it from 王 (king). Highly valued as a symbol of excellence and purity, jade may be found in its crude form, hidden in rough stone. Hence the saying: "Jade which is not chiselled and polished is not an article of beauty."

一	二	千	王	玉								
1	2	3	4	5								

国 guó
country; nation

国宾	guó bīn	state guest
国策	guó cè	national policy
国产	guó chǎn	made in our country
国都	guó dū	national capital
国法	guó fǎ	the law of the land
国防	guó fáng	national defence

国 is composed of 囗 (boundary), - (land), 口 (mouth) and 戈 (spear). 国 therefore means land, people and weapons within a boundary - a country. The simplified form puts only 玉 (jade, representing king) within the boundary (囗) to produce nation: 国 . But a king needs subjects as much as subjects need food: "People are the nation's source; food is the primary need of the people."

丨	冂	冂	冃	冎	囯	国	国					
1	2	3	4	5	6	7	8					

现

xiàn
appear;
reveal;
now

现场	xiàn chǎng	scene (of an incident)
现成	xiàn chéng	ready-made
现代	xiàn dài	modern times; the contemporary age
现款	xiàn kuǎn	ready money; cash

The radical is 玉 (jade, gem) contracted to 王. The phonetic 见, representing eyes (目) of man (儿) means to see. So 现 means the sight of a sparkling gem, its appearance at that very moment; now. Appearances may he revealing or deceptive. According to the saying: "Fine words and appearance are seldom associated with virtue."

一	二	干	王	刊	玑	现	现							
1	2	3	4	5	6	7	8							

理

lǐ

book;
writings

理性	lǐ xìng	reason
理由	lǐ yóu	reason; ground argument
理发	lǐ fà	haircut; hairdressing
理想	lǐ xiǎng	ideal
理智	lǐ zhì	reason; intellect

玉 (gem) is the radical, and the phonetic 里 is made up of 田 (field) and 土 (land). 理 compares the cutting of a gem to the dividing of field and land, both done according to fixed rules and principles; hence the extended meaning: reason, principle. The old saying highlights the importance of a moral standard: "A man of talent without principle is inferior to a simpleton with principle."

一	二	干	王	刊	玑	玑	珇	珇	理	理			
1	2	3	4	5	6	7	8	9	10	11			

主

zhǔ

owner;
master

主办	zhǔ bàn	direct; sponsor
主持	zhǔ chí	chair (a discussion); host (a banquet)
主动	zhǔ dòng	initiative
主队	zhǔ duì	home team; host team
主妇	zhǔ fù	housewife; hostess

主 is a pictograph of a lampstand with the flame rising above it. It symbolises a man who spreads light - a lord or master. To shed light, the master himself needs the enlightening counsel: "If you suspect a man, don't employ him; if you employ a man, don't suspect him."

丶	二	三	辛	主									
1	2	3	4	5									

住 zhù
live;
reside;
stay

住户	zhù hù	household; resident
住口	zhù kǒu	shut up; stop talking
住手	zhù shǒu	stay one's hand; stop
住宿	zhù sù	stay; put up; get accommodation

人 (man) is combined with 主 (master) to form 住 meaning to dwell. In ancient days, the man (人) was always master (主) of his dwelling; so the combination 住 suggests to dwell, to stay. In modern times, however, some husbands still boss the house; others house the boss.

ノ	イ	イ´	个	住	住	住								
1	2	3	4	5	6	7								

全 quán
complete;
perfect

全部	quán bù	whole; complete; total; all
全才	quán cái	a versatile person; all arounder
全场	quán chǎng	the whole audience; all those present

This character was first written 仝 or 全 combining 亼 (joined) with 工 (work). It means completed, i.e., the components are assembled and the work finished. However, the modern character, classified under 入 (In), could be interpreted as a jade (王 or 玉) skilfully inlaid (入), and so flaw less and perfect: 全 . But perfection is not always the crucial thing: "Better an imperfect jade than a perfect tile."

ノ	入	人	仐	仝	全									
1	2	3	4	5	6									

米 mǐ
rice
(uncooked)

米波	mǐ bō	metric wave
米粉	mǐ fěn	rice-flour noodles; vermicelli
米酒	mǐ jiǔ	rice wine
米粒	mǐ lì	gain of rice
米色	mǐ sè	cream-coloured
米制	mǐ zhì	the metric system

米 is a pictograph of a rice stalk. Its original form depicted nine grains of rice ⁛ . This was modified to 米 and finally 米, symbolising grains (⁖) separated in the four quarters (十) by threshing. Although the rice-bowl may represent an honest means of living, "rice obtained by crookedness will not boil up into good food."

、	ヽ`	丷	半	米	米									
1	2	3	4	5	6									

qì
breath;
vapour;
air

气喘	qì chuǎn	asthma
气氛	qì fēn	atmosphere
气愤	qì fèn	indignant; furious
气候	qì hòu	climate
气力	qì lì	effort; energy
气球	qì qiú	balloon
气温	qì wēn	air temperature

气 represents curling vapours rising and forming clouds. Ancient forms show the sun (☉) and fire (火) which cause the vapours: 氣. The regular form 氣, however, depicts the vapour (气) ascending from boiling rice (米) now simplified to 气 , meaning air, vapour, breath, energy or anger.

ノ	一	二	气						
1	2	3	4	5					

---

bǎo
eat to the
full

饱含	bǎo hán	filled with
饱和	bǎo hé	saturation
饱满	bǎo mǎn	full; plump
饱学	bǎo xué	learned

包 the phonetic combines with 食 , the radical for food, to form 飽 (satiated). The seal form of 包 is 包, depicting a foetus enclosed in the body; hence the meaning wrapped up. 飽 therefore means food all wrapped up in the stomach, i.e., fully satisfied. However, as the saying goes: "Better be hungry and pure than well-filled and corrupt."

ノ	𠂉	饣	饣	饣	饣	饣	饱		
1	2	3	4	5	6	7	8		

ě
hungry

挨饿	āi è	go hungry
饥饿	jī è	hunger; starvation

This character is based on the radical for food: 食 . It literally means feed (食) me (我) - a fitting sign for hunger. Another character for hunger is 饑 , literally: little (幾) food (食) simplified to 饥 , i.e., food (饣) on small table (几). Although hunger is no respecter of persons, "Even a hungry person will refuse food offered in contempt."

ノ	𠂉	饣	饣	饣	饣	饿	饿	饿	饿
1	2	3	4	5	6	7	8	9	10

馆

guǎn
hotel; restaurant

旅馆	lǚ guǎn	hotel
美术馆	měi shù guǎn	art gallery
体育馆	tǐ yù guǎn	gymnasium; stadium
图书馆	tú shū guǎn	library

The food radical 食 combines with 官 to produce 馆, a public building. The phonetic 官 (official) originally meant the residence of an official - the hall (宀) of the city (官). 食 (food) together with this suggests a public building doing food business - inn, hotel or restaurant. Hence: "An innkeeper never worries if your appetite is big."

ノ	⺈	⻊	⻌	⻌	饣	饣	馆	馆	馆	馆
1	2	3	4	5	6	7	8	9	10	11

饮

yǐn
drink

饮茶	yǐn chá	drink tea
饮弹	yǐn dàn	be hit by a bullet
饮恨	yǐn hèn	nurse a grievance
饮料	yǐn liào	drink; beverage
饮泣	yǐn qì	weep in silence
饮食	yǐn shí	food and drink; diet

Based on the food radical 食, this character has a significant phonetic 欠, suggesting breath. 欠 originally was a pictograph of a man opening his mouth to catch his breath, as in drinking. This was modified to representing air waves emanating from the man (儿). The primitive form of the character for drink shows clearly a drinking flask (酉) as part of the food radical.

ノ	⺈	⻊	饣	饣	饣	饮				
1	2	3	4	5	6	7				

车

chē
cart; carriage; chariot

車 represents a bird's eye view of a cart, showing its body (田) the two wheels (二) and the axle (丨). The primitive forms of 車 are as varied as carts, carriages and chariots. But, whatever the form, where there is a cart in front there is a track behind; so "Take warning from the wrecked cart ahead of you."

汽车	qì chē	motor vehicle; automobile
车床	chē chuáng	lathe
车费	chē fèi	fare
车祸	chē huò	road accident
车间	chē jiān	workshop
车辆	chē liàng	vehicle; car

一	土	车	车							
1	2	3	4							

hōng
bang;
boom (noise;
uproar)

轰动	hōng dòng	cause a sensation; make a stir
轰击	hōng jī	shell; bombard
轰隆	hōng lōng	rumble; roll
轰鸣	hōng míng	thunder; roar
轰炸	hōng zhà	bomb

轟 is the triple form of the noisy cart (車). It serves as a fitting symbol for any loud or explosive sound like the rumbling of many carts. In the simplified form, 又 (again; ditto) replaces each of the two lower carts to produce 轰 . 又 itself is a simplified picture of the right hand; and the right hand, returning repeatedly to the mouth In eating, suggests "again".

一	七	专	车	车	专	去	轰						
1	2	3	4	5	6	7	8						

kù
storehouse

军械库	jūn xiè kù	armoury
仓库	cāng kù	storehouse; warehouse
库藏	kù cáng	have in storage
库存	kù cún	stock; reserve
库房	kù fáng	storehouse

Just as 宀 is a picture of a roof, representing hut, so 广 Is half a hut - a shed or shop with an open front. 庫 originally was a shed (广) for carts (車). But, before long, It came to be used for storing grain and all sorts of goods. Hence (库) a storehouse, warehouse, granary or depot.

、	宀	广	户	庄	庄	库							
1	2	3	4	5	6	7							

lún
wheel

轮班	lún bān	in shifts; in relays
轮齿	lún chǐ	teeth of a cogwheel
轮船	lún chuán	steamer
轮渡	lún dù	ferry
轮换	lún huàn	rotate; take turns
轮机	lún jī	turbine
轮胎	lún tāi	tyre

輪 the wheel that moves the cart, has 車 (cart) for radicaL. 侖, its phonetic, is suggestive, not only of the orderly arrangement of ~ the spokes of a wheel, but also their unity and stability. It signifies a collection (亼) of ancient documents preserved on bamboo slips tied together in an orderly manner (冊).

一	土	车	车	轩	轮	轮	轮						
1	2	3	4	5	6	7	8						

jūn
army;
soldiers

军备	jūn bèi	armament; arms
军部	jūn bù	army headquarters
军操	jūn cāo	military drill
军车	jūn chē	military vehicle
军队	jūn duì	armed forces
军法	jūn fǎ	military riminal
		code
军港	jūn gǎng	naval port

The seal form of this character shows a war chariot (車) escorted by a surrounding force of soldiers (冖) - an army: 軍. Armies are maintained for years, to be used on a single day. And on that crucial day: "The conquerors are crowned kings; the defeated are branded bandits."

| ' | 冖 | 冖 | 军 | 军 | 军 |
| 1 | 2 | 3 | 4 | 5 | 6 |

zhǎn
chop off

斩断	zhǎn duàn	chop off
斩首	zhǎn shǒu	behead;
		decapitate

斩 probably has reference to a war chariot (車) with warriors wielding axes (斤) to cut off the enemy. It may also mean to whirl or brandish (車) a battle axe (斤). But cutting off an enemy does not eradicate the source of trouble; hence the saying: "When cutting the weeds, get rid of the root" (斩草除根).

| 一 | 士 | 车 | 车 | 车 | 斩 | 斩 | 斩 |
| 1 | 2 | 3 | 4 | 5 | 6 | 7 | 8 |

jiào
sedan-chair

轿车	jiào chē	car
轿子	jiào zi	sedan chair
花轿	huā jiào	bridal sedan chair

轿 is composed of 車 (vehicle) and 喬, something high and stately - the sedan chair. The phonetic 喬 combines 夭 (man leaning forward) with a contracted form of 高 (high). Although the high and mighty travel in sedans, "He who rides in the chair is a man; he who carries the chair is also a man."

| 一 | 士 | 车 | 车 | 车 | 轩 | 轩 | 轿 | 轿 | 轿 |
| 1 | 2 | 3 | 4 | 5 | 6 | 7 | 8 | 9 | 10 |

软 **ruǎn**

soft; weak; pliable; yielding

软钢	ruǎn gāng	mild steel; soft steel
软骨头	ruǎn gú tou	a weak kneed person; a spineless person; a coward
软骨	ruǎn gǔ	cartilage
软化	ruǎn huà	soften; win over by soft tactics

The mobility of the carriage (车) is used to good effect in this character. Combined with 欠, it produces 软, meaning soft and weak or pliable and flexible, 欠 signifying a man (儿) gasping for breath (彡), i.e., exhausted, deficient. 软 may also be written 輭, the phonetic 耎 representing the soft beard (而) of a man (大).

一 𠂇 车 车 𨦋 𨦋 𨦋 软
1 2 3 4 5 6 7 8

连 **lián**

link; join; connect

连忙	lián máng	promptly; at once
连日	lián rì	for days on end; day after day
连同	lián tóng	together with; along with
连续	lián xù	continous; successive

Carts (车) on the move (辶) form a connecting link (連) between places, leaving a continuous track, not broken like the track of man. (連) also represents a string of carriages (車) moving along (辶) as if connected. By the same token 鏈, the character for chain, is made up of rings of metal 金 linked (連) together.

一 𠂇 车 车 连 连 连
1 2 3 4 5 6 7

莲 **lián**

lotus

莲花	lián huā	lotus flower
莲蓬	lián péng	seedpod of the lotus
莲子	lián zi	lotus seed

莲 the lotus, is a prolific water plant (艹) that spreads continuously (連) like a flowery chain. It epitomises purity because it grows out of mud but remains undefiled. From 連 (connect) also comes the character 漣 (ripples) based on the water radical 氵 - ripples being a continuous succession (連) of waves.

一 十 艹 艹 芒 芏 莗 荲 莲 莲
1 2 3 4 5 6 7 8 9 10

父 fù
father

父母	fù mǔ	father and mother; parents
父亲	fù qīn	father
父权制	fù quán zhì	patriarchy
父兄	fù xiōng	father and elder brothers; head of a family

The Chinese proverb defines father as "a man who, in praising his son, extols himself'. Accordingly the seal form 𤕟 depicts father as a disciplinarian - the right hand (ㄅ) wielding the rod of authority (|) Eventually the rod is contracted: ㄅ and then broken: 父. Apparently: "It is easy to govern a kingdom but difficult to rule one's family."

ノ	八	ハ	父									
1	2	3	4									

巾 jīn
napkin; towel
handkerchief

巾帼	jīn guó	woman
餐巾	cān jīn	napkin
手巾	shǒu jīn	han towel
头巾	tóu jīn	headdress
围巾	wéi jīn	scarf

巾 is a pictograph of a small piece of cloth used for cleaning, dusting or wiping. In ancient times It was worn, suspended from the girdle. 冂 represents the two extremities of the cloth hangIng (|) from the girdle. ~ forms the radical of a series of characters relating to cloth In general.

㇑	冂	巾										
1	2	3										

布 bù
cloth

布道	bù dào	preach
布丁	bù dīng	pudding
布防	bù fáng	place troops on garrison duty
布告	bù gào	notice; bulletin; proclamation
布谷鸟	bù gǔ niǎo	cuckoo

This character is based on the radical for cloth: 巾 . The phonetic 父 (father) is discernible as ㄅ in the seal form 𢂷. ㄅ is a picture of the right hand (ㄅ) with the rod of authority (|), and implies discipline, control and order - as essential in weaving as in marrying. So the saying goes: "Hasty weaving produces shoddy cloth; a girl who marries in haste has a fool for a husband."

一	𠂇	𠂇	右	布								
1	2	3	4	5								

zhǒu
broom; duster

扫帚　sào zhǒu　　broom
扫帚星　sào zhǒu xīng　comet

In the seal form 帚, broom is suggested by a hand ( ) with an improvised broom ( ) - double cloth ( ) attached to a handle (|) Although a helping hand (扌) can easily turn 帚 (broom) into 掃 (sweep), "no one will sweep a public hall used by everyone."

┐	㇕	㋤	㋾	录	帚	帚	帚								
1	2	3	4	5	6	7	8								

fù
wife; married woman

少妇　shào fù　　young married woman
夫妇　fū fù　　husband and wife
妇产科　fù chǎn kē　(department of) gynaecology and obstetrics
妇女　fù nǚ　　woman

Woman (女) with broom (帚) is the symbol for wife or married woman: 婦, simplified to 妇 - woman (女) with helping hand (彐). Another character for wife is 妻 - woman (女) with broom (十) in hand (彐). Whatever the character, "She who is the wife of one man cannot eat the rice of two."

く	乆	女	妇	妇	妇										
1	2	3	4	5	6										

dì
emperor

皇帝　huáng dì　emperor
上帝　shàng dì　God
帝国　dì guó　empire
帝王　dì wáng　emperor; monarch
帝制　dì zhì　autocratic monarchy; monarchy

Creating a symbol to suit the emperor can be a thorny problem. The ancient forms 帝 and 帝 represented him with long robes and designated by - (上, superior). Two arms were later added: 帝. Then the bottom was changed to 朿 (朿, thorns) to produce 帝 and finally 帝. Hence the saying: "To attend on the emperor is like sleeping with a tiger."

、	亠	亠	产	产	产	产	帝	帝							
1	2	3	4	5	6	7	8	9							

带 dài

girdle;
bring

录音带	lù yīn dài	recording tape
热带	rè dài	the tropics
带累	dài lěi	implicate; involve
带领	dài lǐng	lead; guide
带路	dài lù	show the way act as a giode

带 is a pictograph of the ancient girdle, embellished with trinkets hanging from it: 丗 . At the bottom of the character are the robes, represented by 帀 - two 巾, one over the other. 带 also means to bring or take along, as articles are often carried, tucked in or worn at the girdle.

一	十	卄	卅	丗	丗	带	带	带				
1	2	3	4	5	6	7	8	9				

帽 mào

hat;
cap

帽徽	mào huī	insignia on a cap
帽子	mào zi	headgear; hat; cap; label; tag; brand

The phonetic 冒 means rash, acting with eyes (目) covered (冃). 冃 indicates a cover (冂) for something (二), viz. the head (二). 冒 combines with the radical 巾 (cloth) to produce 帽 (hat, cap). A cap does not always fit the head of the wearer because "many a good man can be found under a shabby hat."

ノ	冂	巾	巾	帄	帄	帽	帽	帽	帽	帽	帽	
1	2	3	4	5	6	7	8	9	10	11	12	

常 cháng

always;
constantly

常会	cháng huì	regular meeting
常见	cháng jiàn	common
常年	cháng nián	throught the year; perennial
常人	cháng rén	man in the street
常用	cháng yòng	in common use
常驻	cháng zhù	resident; permanent

常 is made up of the radical 巾 (cloth) and phonetic 尚 (elevated). 尚 is a picture of the upper part of a house with a roof (冖) a smoke hole (口) and a ridge (丨) which divides (八) wind and rain. 尚 represents the banner raised as a signal in front of the general's head-quarters and which flies constantly: 常 .

⼂	⼃	⺌	⺌	尚	尚	常	常	常	常	常		
1	2	3	4	5	6	7	8	9	10	11		

bāng
help;
assist

帮忙	bāng máng	help; give a hand; do a favour
帮手	bāng shou	helper; assistant
帮凶	bāng xiōng	accomplice; accessary
帮助	bāng zhù	help; assist

In feudal times the emperor relied on the support of his nobles. The seal form of the eharacter for such aid combines 𡉚 with 帛. 𡉚 denotes the crops (㞢) and land (土) under the noble's rule (彐). 帛 signifies the silk or wealth donated.
In the modern form the phonetic 邦 means state or country represented by woods (丰) and city (阝).

一	二	三	丰	邦	邦	帮	帮	帮
1	2	3	4	5	6	7	8	9

yī
clothes

衣橱	yī chú	wardrobe
衣服	yī fu	clothing; clothes
衣架	yī jià	coat hanger; clothes-rack
衣鱼	yī yú	silverfish; fish mouth; bookworm

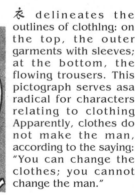

衣 delineates the outlines of clothing: on the top, the outer garments with sleeves; at the bottom, the flowing trousers. This pictograph serves asa radical for characters relating to clothing Apparently, clothes do not make the man, according to the saying: "You can change the clothes; you cannot change the man."

丶	一	亠	𠂇	衣	衣
1	2	3	4	5	6

kù
trousers

| 短裤 | duǎn kù | shorts |
| 裤子 | kù zi | trousers; pants |

裤 meaning trousers, is based on the radical 衣 (clothing). The ample storage space of loose Chinese trousers is suggested by the phonetic 库 (store). 裤 may also be written: 袴, the phonetic 夸 meaning big (大) talk or exclamation (亏).
衫 or robe, the other basic article of clothing (衣) is likened to feathers (彡) that warm the body.

丶	𠃌	才	礻	衤	衤	衤	衤	裤	裤	裤	裤
1	2	3	4	5	6	7	8	9	10	11	12

bèi
bedclothes; blankets

被捕	bèi bǔ	be arrested; be
被单	bèi dān	(bed) sheet
被动	bèi dòng	passive
被俘	bèi fú	be captured; be taken prisoner
被告	bèi gào	defendant; the accused

被 bedclothes or blankets, are regarded as cloth (衣) skin (皮). The phonetic 皮 or 𠬝, represents the skin (㇇) flayed by hand (㇇) with knife (㇇). 被 may also mean to suffer, a sign of the passive. However, 袍 (literally, cloth 衣 wrap 包) refers to the long robe or outer garment wrapped round the body to keep it warm and active.

`	㇇	㇇	衤	衤	衤	衤	袻	被	被
1	2	3	4	5	6	7	8	9	10

biǎo
express; show; manifest

表层	biǎo céng	surface layer
表达	biǎo dá	express; convey; voice
表决	biǎo jué	decide by vote; vote
表露	biǎo lù	show reveal
表面	biǎo miàn	surface; face

表 combining 衣 with 毛, means to show or make known. Clothes (衣) were originally skins with hair (毛) on the outside. 表 literally means the outside of clothes - the manifestation or outer appearance which may be a false front. It is said that when a boy is small you can see the man, but "A man cannot be known by his looks, nor can the sea be measured with a bushel basket."

一	二	𦍌	圭	声	表	表	表
1	2	3	4	5	6	7	8

piàn
slice; piece

片段	piàn duàn	part; passage; extract; fragment
片刻	piàn kè	a short while; an instant; a moment
片时	piàn shí	a short while; a moment

Man cannot wait to saw a tree (木) vertically into two halves: 爿 and 片. 爿 serves as a strong plank for his bed and 片 as a symbol for a slice or piece. With 爿 and 片 he forms a tripod for an urn: 鼎 . He uses 木 and its components 爿 and 片 as radicals. And so the saying goes: "He plants a tree in the morning and wants to saw planks from it in the evening."

丿	丿	丬	片
1	2	3	4

床 chuáng
bed

单人床	dān rén chuáng	single bed
双人床	shuāng rén chuáng	double bed
床单	chuáng dān	bedsheet
床垫	chuáng diàn	mattress
床位	chuáng wèi	berth; bunk; bed
床罩	chuáng zhào	bedspread

爿 the left half of a tree (木) represents a thick, strong plank used for a bed. By adding 爿 to 木 you can make 牀 (bed) - literally, strong plank (爿) of wood (木). Another way is by placing 木 (wood) under 广 (roof): 床 . As you make your bed, you must lie on it, so "if you can't sleep, don't complain about your bed."

、	一	广	广	庐	庄	床							
1	2	3	4	5	6	7							

墙 qiáng
wall

墙壁	qiáng bì	wall
墙角	qiáng jiǎo	a corner formed by two walls
墙脚	qiáng jiǎo	the foot of a wall; foundation

The seal form of the phonetic 嗇 signifies grain 來 stored within (入) a double-walled granary (回) The idea of wall is reinforced by the radical 爿, a symbol of strength. Since walls are made of clay or earth (土), the character may also be written: 墻 . Walls may fortify a city, but "men, not walls, make a city."

一	十	土	圹	圹	圹	圹	墒	墒	墙	墙	墙	墙	墙
1	2	3	4	5	6	7	8	9	10	11	12	13	14

将 jiāng
take; hold; handle; shall; will

将近	jiāng jìn	close to; nearly; almost
将军	jiāng jūn	general
将来	jiāng lái	future

将 has many seal forms and varied meanings:
牉 is a meat block (爿) with meat (肉)
牉 shows the meatblock (爿) with meat (爫) and salt (鹵)
牉 represents the meatblock (爿) with meat (爫) and brine (酉)
牉 signifies the hand (寸) placing meat (爫) upon the block
Hence the extended meanings: offer, present; nourish, help; take, hold; handle, manage. 将 is a character with a future, often used for shall or will; it is even used to mean leader or general.

、	二	丬	丬	丬	丬	丬	将	将					
1	2	3	4	5	6	7	8	9					

壮 zhuàng

strong;
eminent;
impressive

壮胆	zhuàng dǎn	embolden; boost somebody's courage
壮丽	zhuàng lì	majestic; magnificent
壮烈	zhuàng liè	heroic; brave
壮士	zhuàng shì	hero; warrior
壮实	zhuàng shi	sturdy; robust

壮 literally means a strong and impressive (爿) personage (士) or one who professes to be so; by extension, strong and able-bodied. An analogous character is 妆 (adorn, disguise) - an impressive (爿) woman (女), i.e., one who adorns herself with make-up.

丶	丷	爿	丬	壮	壮						
1	2	3	4	5	6						

装 zhuāng

pack;
fill;
pretend

装扮	zhuāng bàn	dress up; disguise
装备	zhuāng bèi	equip; equipment; outfit
装胡涂	zhuāng hú tu	pretend not to know
装货	zhuāng huò	loading (cargo)
装甲车	zhuāng jiǎ chē	armoured car

壮 the phonetic, means strong or robust. It was originally, concerned with appearance. The addition of the radical 衣 (clothing) suggests putting oneself in another's clothing and filling it - to deceive; by extension, to pack, fill, pretend: 装 .

丶	丷	爿	丬	壮	壮	壮	壯	荸	茅	装	装
1	2	3	4	5	6	7	8	9	10	11	12

夕 xī

evening

夕烟	xī yān	evening mist
夕阳	xī yáng	the setting sun
夕照	xī zhào	the glow of the setting the glow of the setting sun; evening glow

夕 is a picture of the crescent moon emerging on the horizon at dusk, its lower part obstructed by a mountain. Hence the extended meaning: dusk, evening. To man the rising moon presents opportunities but the proverb laments. How seldom in life is the moon directly overhead!"

丿	夕	夕									
1	2	3									

多 duō
many; much

多半 　duō bàn 　the greater part; most
多方面 duō fāng miàn many-sided; in many ways
多民族 duō mín zú 　multinational
多余 　duō yú 　unnecessary; superfluous

From morning to evening man toiled in the field, and evening (夕) after evening (夕) he noted the fruitage of his labour. "Many evenings" (多) soon came to mean "many". His hard work bore much (多) fruit (果), producing a new word: 夥 (fruitful) and demonstrating the principle: "Sow much, reap much; sow little, reap little."

ノ	ク	タ	夕	多	多						
1	2	3	4	5	6						

够 gòu
enough

够本 　gòu běn 　break even
够朋友 gòu péng you be a friend indeed
够受的 gòu shòu de quite an ordeal
够意思 gòu yì si really something; terrific; generous; really kind

句 is to hook (勹) with the mouth (口) to entice; 多 means much many. 够 therefore signifies to entice many, i.e., enough. But enough is not always enough, according to the proverb: "To complete a thing a hundred years is not sufficient, to destroy it, a day is more than enough."

ノ	勹	勹	句	句	句	句	够	够	够	够	
1	2	3	4	5	6	7	8	9	10	11	

外 wài
outside

外币 wài bì 　foreign currency
外边 wài bian 　outside; out
外表 wài biǎo 　outward appearance; exterior
外宾 wài bīn 　foreign guest
外公 wài gōng 　(maternal) grandfather

外 is composed of 夕 (evening) and 卜 (divine). Divination (卜) by interpreting the vertical (|) and horizontal (-) cracks of a heated tortoise-shell, was deemed effective only before (or outside of) evening. Hence the meaning: outside or foreign. And for such outside or foreign help, many will pay handsomely - those who place trust in the saying: "Much money moves the gods."

ノ	ク	タ	列	外							
1	2	3	4	5							

梦 **mèng**
dream

梦话	mèng huà	words uttered in one's sleep; somniloquy
梦幻	mèng huàn	illusion; dream; reverie
梦境	mèng jìng	dreamland; dreamworld; dream

The seal forms of dream are horrifying enough to evoke a nightmare. No wonder the original character; 瞢 means bad sight (苜) with covered (冂) eyes (目). Dreams being evening visions, 夕 replaces 目 in the new form: 夢, now simplified to 梦 (evening trees) - a pleasant dream. Unfortunately, "a beautiful dream is soon ended."

一	十	才	木	木	村	材	林	梦	梦	梦									
1	2	3	4	5	6	7	8	9	10	11									

夜 **yè**
night

开夜车	kāi yè chē	work deep into the night; burn the midnight oil
夜班	yè bān	night shift
夜半	yè bàn	midnight
夜工	yè gōng	night job
夜盲	yè máng	night blindness

The seal character 夜 depicts man (大) sleeping on his side (丿) in the evening (夕). The modern form 夜 shows man (亻) under cover (亠) lying on his other side (乀) also in the evening (夕). If night can be suggested by sleep, as in both these forms, then day can be transformed into night, as demonstrated by our sleepy characters shown here.

`	一	广	疒	疒	夜	夜	夜												
1	2	3	4	5	6	7	8												

从 **cóng**
follow; from

从容	cóng róng	calm; unhurried; leisurely
从此	cóng cǐ	from this time on; henceforth
从简	cóng jiǎn	conform to the principle of simplicity

從 represents two men (从) walking (彳) and stopping (止). In the seal form, 彳 and 止 are united into 辵 (going). The simplified form is 从 - a man following another man - a simple task, in view of the saying: "To know the truth is easy; but, ah, how difficult it is to follow it!"

丿	人	㐅	从																
1	2	3	4																

得 dé
get; obtain

得到	dé dào	get; obtain; gain; receive
得分	dé fēn	score
得奖	dé jiǎng	win or be awarded a prize
得胜	dé shèng	win a victory; triumph
得益	dé yì	benefit; profit

彳, the radical, means step. The phonetic 㝵 to lay hands (寸) on what one has in view (見 or 罒) - signifies to obtain. However, laying hands on money not easy: "Money comes like earth picked up with a pin, but goes like sand washed away by water."

ノ	⺆	彳	彳	彳⁷	彳⁷	彳⁷	彳⁷	得	得	得
1	2	3	4	5	6	7	8	9	10	11

德 dé
virtue; goodness

德国	Dé Guó	Germany
德行	dé xíng	moral integrity; moral conduct
德育	dé yù	moral education
品德	pǐng dé	moral character

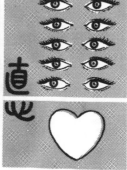

直 means straight (一) as tested by ten (十) eyes (目). 心 is the heart So the phonetic 惪 denotes a straight heart. Clarified by the radical for step (彳) to mean the way to virtue or goodness, 德 is defined by the saying: "To talk good is not being good; to do good, that is being good."

ノ	⺆	彳	彳	彳	彳	彳	彳	德	德	德	德	德	德	德
1	2	3	4	5	6	7	8	9	10	11	12	13	14	15

律 lǜ
law; rule discipline

| 律吕 | lǜ lǚ | bamboo pitch-pitch-pipes used in ancient china; temperament |
| 律师 | lǜ shī | lawyer; barrister; solicitor |

The phonetic 聿 signifies written regulations - hand (彐) with pen (丨) writing lines (一) on tablet (一). The radical 彳 (step) suggests steps taken to enforce them as law to protect the citizens. However, "Going to the law is losing a cow for the sake of a cat."

ノ	⺆	彳	彳	彳	彳	律	律	律
1	2	3	4	5	6	7	8	9

待 dài
treat;
deal with

待命	dài mìng	await orders
待续	dài xù	to be continued
待遇	dài yù	treatment; remuneration

寺 is a court where the law or rule (寸) is applied continually, like the growth of a plant (彳) The radical 彳 indicates the step or way to treat others with propriety, requiring patience and application of the golden rule: "Do to others as you would have them do to you."

ノ	ク	イ	彳	彳	往	往	待	待											
1	2	3	4	5	6	7	8	9											

功 gōng
merit;
achievement

功德	gōng dé	merits and virtues
功课	gōng kè	schoolwork; homework
功劳	gōng láo	contribution; meritorious service; credit
功能	gōng néng	function

Strength (力) is here symbolized by muscles, and work (工) by a carpenter's square. Strength exerted in work produces 功 - merit or achievement. On the other hand, little (少) strength (力) results in 劣 , meaning bad or inferior.

一	T	工	功	功															
1	2	3	4	5															

加 jiā
add;
increase

加班	jiā bān	work overtime
加倍	jiā bèi	double; redouble
加法	jiā fǎ	addition
加害	jiā hài	injure; do harm to
加紧	jiā jǐn	step up; speed up; intensify
加宽	jiā kuān	broaden; widen

This ideograph means to add to or increase. It adds strength (力) to mouth (口) by applying force to words. Adding violence to persuasion cannot always be justified. Although might is never right, right is always might.

刁	力	加	加	加															
1	2	3	4	5															

协 xié

together
co-operate

协定	xié dìng	agreement; accord
协会	xié huì	association; society
协力	xié lì	unite efforts; join in a common effort
协商	xié shāng	consult; talk things over

Triple-strength (劦) signifying the multiple efforts of ten (十) persons in unity, indicates wholehearted cooperation: 協. Without cooperation, shared responsibility leads to neglect. "If two men feed a horse, it will be thin, if two men mend a boat, it will leak."

一	十	圤	协	协	协						
1	2	3	4	5	6						

劳 láo

work;
labour

劳动	láo dòng	work; labour
劳工	láo gōng	labourer; worker
劳累	láo lèi	tired; run down
劳力	láo lì	labour force
劳碌	láo lù	work hard; toil

劳 is to toil (力) indoors (冖) by the light of many fires (火火). Burning the midnight oil or the candle at both ends is a waste of effort. "It is labour lost, trying to catch the moon in the water or polishing brick to make a mirror."

一	十	艹	艹	芦	劳	劳					
1	2	3	4	5	6	7					

光 guāng

light;
glory

光彩	guāng cǎi	lustre; splendour; radiance; honourable; glorious
光辐射	guāng fú shè	ray radiation
光顾	guāng gù	patronize
光辉	guāng huī	radiance; brilliance

The ancient form 炗 means twenty (廿) fires (火). The modern form 灮 portrays a man (儿) bearing a torch (火) Whatever the form, 光 means brightness and glory which, unfortunately, never lasts. Hence: "A bright dawn does not always make a fine day."

丨	丬	业	业	光	光						
1	2	3	4	5	6						

先 xiān
first; before

先辈	xiān bèi	elder generation; ancestors
先导	xiān dǎo	guide; forerunner
先后	xiān hòu	early or late; priority one after another
先进	xiān jìn	advanced
先生	xiān sheng	teacher; mister

The top part 生 is a small plant (屮) issuing from the ground (一); thus indicating progress. The lower part is a picture of marching legs. Accordingly, 先 means to advance 生 on one's feet (儿) - to be first. And to progress with people, remember: "Courtesy first, force later" (先礼后兵).

ノ	⺊	牛	生	先	先								
1	2	3	4	5	6								

洗 xǐ
strength; force; power

洗尘	xǐ chén	give a dinner of welcome (to a visitor from afar)
洗涤	xǐ dí	wash cleanse
洗发剂	xǐ fà jì	shampoo
洗劫	xǐ jié	loot; sack
洗澡	xǐ zǎo	have a bath; bathe

The radical is 氵 (water) and the phonetic 先 (first). This suggests that you must have water (氵) first (先) to wash or clean: 洗 . And what needs to be cleansed first? According to the proverbial exhortation: "Cleanse your heart as you would cleanse a dish."

`	⺀	氵	汁	汁	沖	洪	洪	洗					
1	2	3	4	5	6	7	8	9					

海 hǎi
sea; ocean

海岸	hǎi àn	coast; seashore
海豹	hǎi bào	seal
海滨	hǎi bīn	seaside
海产	hǎi chǎn	marine products
海盗	hǎi dào	pirate; sea rover
海港	hǎi gǎng	seaport; harbour
海军	hǎi jūn	navy

母 is a picture of a woman with breasts for suckling a child, signifying mother (母).
每 compares a mother (母) with a sprout (⺊) always reproducing; hence meaning every, always.
海 represents the sea, where there is always (每) plenty of water (氵).

`	⺀	氵	汇	汇	汇	海	海	海	海				
1	2	3	4	5	6	7	8	9	10				

林 lín
forest

艺林	yì lín	art circles
竹林	zhú lín	bamboo grove
林产品	lín chǎn pǐn	forest products
林带	lín dài	forest belt
林立	lín lì	stand in great numbers (like trees in a forest)
林木	lín mù	forest; woods

"A single fibre does not make a thread; a single tree does not make a forest," so goes the saying. The character for tree is a pictograph: 木. Two trees form a company - a grove or forest: 林. Three trees make a crowd, signifying dense or overgrown: 森.

一	十	才	木	朮	杜	材	林						
1	2	3	4	5	6	7	8						

枝 zhī
branch

枝杈	zhī chà	branch; twig
枝接	zhī jiē	scion grafting
		newspapers
枝叶	zhī yè	branches and leaves; non-essentials
枝子	zhī zi	branch; twig

枝 is a branch (支) of a tree (木). 支 itself is a picture of the right hand (又) holding a twig (十) and means branch. Because branches form an integral part of a tree, "One branch moves, a hundred branches shake." 枯 means withered, like an old (古) tree (木) - one that has passed through ten (十) generations or mouths (口).

一	十	才	木	朮	杜	杖	枝						
1	2	3	4	5	6	7	8						

病 bìng
painting; drawing

流行病	liú xíng bìng	epidemic disease
心脏病	xīn zàng bìng	heart trouble; heart disease
病倒	bìng dǎo	be down with an illness; be laid up
病假	bìng jià	sick leave
病态	bìng tài	morbid state

The radical for disease 疒 (疒) is made up of a horizontal line (一) - the position of a sick person - and the bed (爿). The idea of sickness is reinforced by the phonetic 丙 (疚) - fire (火) in the house (宀), referring to high fever. 病 also means defect or fault, and it is said: "A wise doctor never treats himself."

、	二	广	疒	疒	疒	疒	病	病	病				
1	2	3	4	5	6	7	8	9	10				

疼 téng

pain;
ache

| 疼爱 | téng ài | be very fond of |
| 疼痛 | téng tòng | pain; ache; soreness |

Just as fire or fever suggests sickness, winter (冬) or intense cold is here combined with the radical for sickness (疒) to signify pain: 疼 . However, young and old do not feel pain alike. In youth, the absence of pleasure is pain; in old age, the absence of pain is pleasure.

| 、 | 丶 | 广 | 疒 | 疒 | 疒 | 疒 | 疾 | 疾 | 疼 | | | |
| 1 | 2 | 3 | 4 | 5 | 6 | 7 | 8 | 9 | 10 | | | |

疾 jí

disease;
ailment

眼疾	yǎn jí	eye trouble
疾病	jí bìng	disease; illness
疾风	jí fēng	strong wind; gale
疾苦	jí kǔ	sufferings; hardship

Disease strikes suddenly and unexpectedly like an arrow. Hence 疾 , meaning disease, made up of the radical for sickness (疒) and arrow (矢). According to the proverb: "Diseases enter by the mouth; misfortunes issue from it."

| 、 | 丶 | 广 | 疒 | 疒 | 疒 | 疒 | 疒 | 疾 | 疾 | | | |
| 1 | 2 | 3 | 4 | 5 | 6 | 7 | 8 | 9 | 10 | | | |

道 dào

way;
path

首 is a pictograph of a hairy (疾) head (之) and means head or chief. Combined with 辶 or 辵 (go), it produces 道 - the way of virtue. Head (首) and feet (辶) advancing on the same path symbolizes the Tao (道) of which it is said: "To believe in the Tao is easy; to keep the Tao is difficult."

道德	dào dé	morals; morality; ethics
道贺	dào hè	congratulate
道教	Dào Jiào	Taoism
道具	dào jù	stage property; prop

| 、 | 丷 | 丷 | 首 | 首 | 首 | 首 | 首 | 首 | 道 | 道 | 道 | |
| 1 | 2 | 3 | 4 | 5 | 6 | 7 | 8 | 9 | 10 | 11 | 12 | |

miàn
face

面对	miàn duì	face; confront
面对面	miàn duì miàn	facing each other; face-to-face
面粉	miàn fěn	wheat flour; flour
面积	miàn jī	area
面颊	miàn jiá	cheek

This radical incorporates 囗, an outline of the face, with 百 (head) featuring the eyes (目) as its most prominent part. Because a person is identified by his face, we know a man's face, not his mind. Nevertheless, "Be able to say in his face what you say behind his back."

一	一	一	万	而	而	而	面	面						
1	2	3	4	5	6	7	8	9						

---

 xiā
blind

瞎扯	xiā chě	talk irresponsibly; talk rubbish
瞎话	xiā huà	untruth; lie
瞎闹	xiā nào	act senselessly; mess about; fool around; be mischievous

瞎 stands for injured (害) eyes (目). The phonetic 害 (harm) represents injury from a stick (丨) with notches (三) or injury by mouth (口) under cover (宀). Another ideograph for blind is 盲 or lost (亡) eyes (目). Despite their handicap, "The blind are quick at hearing; the deaf are quick at sight."

丨	刀	月	月	目	目丶	目丶	盯	睁	瞎	瞎	睅	瞎	瞎	瞎
1	2	3	4	5	6	7	8	9	10	11	12	13	14	15

---

 shuì
sleep

睡觉	shuì jiào	sleep
睡莲	shuì lián	water lily
睡梦	shuì mèng	sleep; slumber
睡眠	shuì mián	sleep
睡醒	shuì xǐng	wake up
睡衣	shuì yī	night clothes; pyjamas

睡 is to have the eyes or eyelids (目) hanging down (垂) - to sleep. The phonetic 垂 or 坙 depicts a bough loaded with leaves (秝) hanging down towards the earth (土). Sleep, even if your eyes are closed, is not always a peaceful affair. According to the saying, "Attending to the Emperor is like sleeping with a tiger."

丨	刀	月	月	目	目	目	盱	肝	睡	睡	睡	睡		
1	2	3	4	5	6	7	8	9	10	11	12	13		

胃

wèi
stomach

胃病	wèi bìng	stomach trouble; gastric disease
胃口	wèi kǒu	appetite; liking
胃溃疡	wèi kuì yáng	gastric ulcer
胃酸	wèi suān	hydrochloric acid in gastric juice
胃痛	wèi tòng	gastralgia
胃液	wèi yè	gastric juice

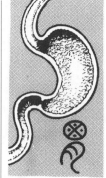

This ideograph combines two pictographs. The upper one is pouch filled with rice: 胃 ; the lower, a piece of flesh: 月. Hence, stomach - a fleshy pouch filled with rice. Although a full stomach begets a contented mind "Better be hungry and pure than well-filled and corrupt."

ノ	门	冂	冃	田	甲	胃	胃	胃				
1	2	3	4	5	6	7	8	9				

思

sī
think

思潮	sī cháo	trend of thought; ideological trend; thoughts
思考	sī kǎo	think deeply; ponder over; reflect on

This ideograph combines the skull (囟) with the heart (心) to produce thought: 思. The faculties of reasoning and feeling are here exercised to create a balanced mind. And, according to the saying, "If you wish to know the mind of a man, listen to his words."

ノ	口	日	囝	田	田	思	思	思				
1	2	3	4	5	6	7	8	9				

情

qíng
feeling; affection

情报	qíng bào	intelligence; information
情操	qíng cāo	sentiment
情敌	qíng dí	rival in love
情调	qíng diào	sentiment; emotional appeal
情感	qíng gǎn	emotion; feeling

青 is green - the colour (丹) of nature and growing plants (生). With the addition of the radical for heart (忄) the character stands for those feelings which are pure or natural to the heart of man: 情. Lamenting the lack of depth and substance in such feelings, the saying goes: "Human feelings are as thin as sheets of paper."

`	忄	忄	忄	忄	忄	情	情	情	情	情		
1	2	3	4	5	6	7	8	9	10	11		

放 fàng
release

放 means to release - to drive out 攵 into an open space or pasture (方). The radical 攵 (攴) is a hand with stick; the phonetic 方 is a square or open space. Horses or cattle released for grazing can always be rounded up, but "Words once released cannot be recaptured by the swiftest steeds."

放出	fàng chū	give out; let out; emit
放大	fàng dà	enlarge; magnify; amplify
放胆	fàng dǎn	act boldly and with confidence
放荡	fàng dàng	dissolute; dissipated

`	一	亠	方	方	於	放	放					
1	2	3	4	5	6	7	8					

政 zhèng
government

The radical 攵 represents the right hand wielding the rod of authority. The phonetic 正 signifies a foot (止) walking the straight way (一). Hence 政 which means government, an upright (正) administration (攵) - an enforcement for good. No wonder the saying goes: "Beasts hate the net as people dislike government."

政变	zhèng biàn	coup d'etat
政策	zhèng cè	policy
政党	zhèng dǎng	political party
政敌	zhèng dí	political opponent
政法	zhèng fǎ	politics and law
政府	zhèng fǔ	government
政客	zhèng kè	politician

一	丁	下	正	正	正	正	政	政				
1	2	3	4	5	6	7	8	9				

叫 jiào
call

叫喊	jiào hǎn	shout; yell; howl
叫好	jiào hǎo	applaud
叫唤	jiào huàn	cry out; call out
叫苦	jiào kǔ	complain of hardship or suffering; moan and groan

叫 is to call out (口) the measure (斗). The ancient form of depicts a measuring ladle (⼅) with ten (十): 卂 . Although vendors shout out their wares, a melon seller never cries "Bitter melons!" nor a wine seller "Thin wine!"

㇑	口	口	叫	叫								
1	2	3	4	5								

听 tīng
hear; listen

听从	tīng cóng	obey; heed; comply with
听话	tīng huà	be obedient
听觉	tīng jué	sense of hearing
听说	tīng shuō	be told; hear of
听写	tīng xiě	dictation
听众	tīng zhòng	audience; listeners

聽 is the rectification (直 or 壬) of the heart (心) of a listener or disciple (壬) by his ear (耳) hence to listen or obey. The simplified form 听 combines 口 (mouth) with 斤 (discerning), i.e., to discern what comes from the mouth - by listening. It may even suggest that most people today listen with their mouths!

㇒	㇆	口	口丶	吖	听	听					
1	2	3	4	5	6	7					

聋 lóng
deaf

聋哑	lóng yǎ	deaf and dumb; deaf-mute
聋子	lóng zi	a deaf person

Because the dragon is king of the supernatural creatures (the others being the unicorn, the phoenix and the tortoise), it can afford to turn a deaf ear to anything. Hence dragon's 龙 ear (耳) meaning deaf: 聋. But let not those who cannot hear well lose heart: "In the kingdom of the deaf, the one-eared man is king!"

一	ナ	尤	龙	龙	龙	耂	耷	耷	聋	聋	
1	2	3	4	5	6	7	8	9	10	11	

喜 xǐ
happiness; pleasure

喜爱	xǐ ài	like; love; be fond of; be keen on
喜欢	xǐ huān	like; love; happy; elated; filled with joy
喜酒	xǐ jiǔ	wedding feast
喜剧	xǐ jù	comedy

喜 or happiness is expressed by 壴 (music) and 口 (singing). 壴 depicts the ancient drum on its stand (豆) with its stretched skin (一) and a straightened right hand (屮) striking it. 口 represents the mouth singing. True happiness, however, comes from unselfish giving; and when you make two people happy, one of them is probably you.

一	十	士	吉	吉	吉	壴	壴	壴	喜	喜	喜
1	2	3	4	5	6	7	8	9	10	11	12

春 chūn
spring

春光	chūn guāng	sights and sounds of spring
春季	chūn jì	spring; springtime
春卷	chūn juǎn	spring roll
春天	chūn tiān	spring; springtime

the seal character for spring (春) signifies the growth and out burst (屯) of vegetation (屮屮) under the influence of the sun (日). As unpredictable and changeable as the weather, spring comes either early or late each year. Hence the proverb: "Spring has a stepmother's face."

一	二	三	丰	夫	表	春	春	春					
1	2	3	4	5	6	7	8	9					

唱 chàng
sing

唱词	chàng cí	libretto; words of a ballad
唱歌	chàng gē	sing (a song)
唱工	chàng gōng	art of singing; singing
唱片	chàng piàn	gramophone record

昌 is composed of 日 (sun) and 曰 (speak). 曰 is the mouth (口) that exhales a breath; by extension, exhalation and emanation. So 昌 means prosperous or splendid, just as the sun sends forth rays and the mouth puts forth words. 唱 therefore refers to singing which produces a more refined quality of the voice than an ordinary conversation.

丨	冂	口	叭	叨	叩	吅	吕	唱	唱	唱		
1	2	3	4	5	6	7	8	9	10	11		

歌 gē
song

歌本	gē běn	song book
歌词	gē cí	words of a song
歌喉	gē hóu	(singer's) voice
歌剧	gē jù	opera
歌谱	gē pǔ	music of a song

可 is an exclamation of approval (丁) from the mouth (口) and means can or may.
哥 is 可 doubled, suggesting singing, now used for addressing elder brother by sound loan.
歌 adds breath (欠) to singing (哥) to produce a song.

一	丆	可	可	可	叴	叧	哥	哥	哥	哥	歌	歌	歌
1	2	3	4	5	6	7	8	9	10	11	12	13	14

如 rú
like; as

如常	rú cháng	as usual
如此	rú cǐ	so; such; in this way
如果	rú guǒ	if; in case; in the event of
如何	rú hé	how; what
如今	rú jīn	nowadays; now

Ideographically, 如 is to speak (口) like or as a woman (女) that is, appropriately to the circumstances and the disposition of the man she desires to influence. Testifying to such persuasive, womanly skill is the saying: "The walls of a city are raised by men's wisdom but overthrown by women's wiles."

く	夕	女	如	如	如						
1	2	3	4	5	6						

客 kè
guest; visitor

客船	kè chuán	passenger ship
客串	kè chuàn	be a guest performer
客队	kè duì	(sports) visiting team
客房	kè fáng	guest room
客观	kè guān	objective

夂 represents a man following his own way.
各 signifies his going his way (夂) without heeding advice (口); by extension, each or every.
客 is a guest - one who has his way under another's roof (宀). No wonder "the host is happy when the guest is gone."

`	宀	宀	宀	夂	安	安	客	客			
1	2	3	4	5	6	7	8	9			

比 bǐ
compare

比方	bǐ fang	analogy; instance
比分	bǐ fēn	score
比价	bǐ jià	price relations; parity; rate of exchange
比率	bǐ ù	ratio; rate
比赛	bǐ sài	match; competition

The seal form of 比 reveals this character as an inverted form of 从 (follow). It represents two men standing as if to compare heights. "When compared with those above," so goes the saying, "there is something lacking; but compared with those below, there is something to spare."

一	上	上	比								
1	2	3	4								

背 bèi

back; oppose
carry on the back

背痛	bèi tòng	backache
背地里	bèi dì li	behind somebody's back; privately; on the sly
背后	bèi hòu	behind; at the back; in the car
背脊	bèi jǐ	the back of the human body

A person sitting facing the south (as is the custom) and back to back with another suggests north: 北. Turning one's back on another signifies opposition. Hence 背, referring to the back (北) of the body (月), may mean to oppose or to carry on the back.

㇒	十	丬	孑	北	北	背	背	背				
1	2	3	4	5	6	7	8	9				

凶 xiōng

unfortunate;
ominous

凶残	xiōng cán	fierce and cruel; savage and cruel
凶恶	xiōng è	fierce, ferocious; fiendish
凶猛	xiōng měng	violent; ferocious
凶杀	xiōng shā	homicide; murder

凶 (Ⓧ) means unfortunate, symbolized by a man falling upside down (✗) into a pit (凵). Calamities do not always come by accident. According to the proverb, "Calamity comes by means of the mouth."

㇒	ㄨ	凶	凶									
1	2	3	4									

答 dá

reply;
answer

答案	dá àn	answer; solution; key
答辩	dá biàn	reply (to a charge, query or an argument)
答复	dá fù	answer; reply

Because of its beauty, design and harmony (合) the bamboo (竹) is used here as a perfect example of an answer or reply: 答. However, like bamboos, answers come in various lengths. Many a short question is evaded by a long answer.

㇒	㇑	㇒	处	竹	竹	竹	炊	答	答	答	答	
1	2	3	4	5	6	7	8	9	10	11	12	

篮 lán
basket

投篮	tóu lán	(basketball) shoot a basket
篮球	lán qiú	basketball
篮圈	lán quān	(basketball) ring; hoop
篮子	lán zi	basket

皿 is to bend over (臥) a full vase (血) to examine its contents; by extension, to oversee those who are confined in a prison. When the bamboo radical 竹 is added, we have a bamboo container to confine goods for safe transportation - a basket: 籃 now simplified to 篮.

| ノ | ⺮ | ⺮ | 竹 | 竹 | 竹 | 竿 | 竿 | 笁 | 笁 | 筮 | 篮 | 篮 | 篮 | 篮 | 篮 |
|1|2|3|4|5|6|7|8|9|10|11|12|13|14|15|16|

井 jǐng
well

矿井	kuàng jǐng	pit; mine
油井	yóu jǐng	oil well; neat; orderly
井场	jǐng cháng	well site
井架	jǐng jià	derrick

Originally the seal form 井 represented fields divided among eight families, with the well in the middle plot to serve the public. The well also serves to expose man's inclination to faultfinding: "One does not blame the shortness of the rope, but the deepness of the well."

| 一 | 二 | 丰 | 井 |
|1|2|3|4|

石 shí
stone

石斑鱼	shí bān yú	grouper
石壁	shí bì	cliff; precipice
石雕	shí diāo	stone carving; carved stonc
石膏	shí gāo	gypsum; plaster stone

石 is a picture of a piece of stone or rock (口) falling from a cliff (厂). 岩 is a steep rock (石) or cliff that looks like a hill (山). The rock, being strong, symbolizes integrity. Hence: "Slander cannot destroy an honest man; when the flood recedes the rock appears."

| 一 | 丆 | 才 | 石 | 石 |
|1|2|3|4|5|

xiān
fairy; recluse

仙丹	xiān dān	elixir of life
仙姑	xiān gū	female immortal; sorceress
仙鹤	xiān hè	red-crowned crane
仙境	xiān jìng	fairyland; wonderland; paradise
仙人掌	xiān rén zhǎng	cactus

The ancient form 僊 signifies a human (人) who rises by climbing with his head (囟) and four hands (𦥑) probably after the manner of a monkey. An official seal (卪) is added to denote promotion. The modern form 仙 associates person (亻) with mountain (山), suggesting recluse and fairy.

ノ	イ	仈	仙	仙					
1	2	3	4	5					

gāo
high; tall

高傲	gāo ào	supercilious; arrogant
高潮	gāo cháo	high tide; upsurge; climax
高大	gāo dà	tall and big; tall
高度	gāo dù	altitude; height
高贵	gāo guì	noble; high; elitist

高 is a pictograph of a high tower or pavilion 冋 on a lofty sub-structure (冂) equipped with a hall (口). It stands for high. When it comes to position, no person stoops so low as the one most eager to rise high in the world. But beware: "He who climbs too high will have a heavy fall."

丶	亠	宀	亣	高	亨	高	高	高	高
1	2	3	4	5	6	7	8	9	10

jīng
capital city

京城	jīng chéng	the capital of a country
京剧	jīng jù	Beijing opera

京 is derived from 高 (high). It is a contraction of 高 with the lower part replaced by 小, a pivot, conveying the idea of loftiness and centrality. So lofty is the capital city that it is said: "One who can speak, speaks of the city; one who cannot, talks merely of household affairs."

丶	亠	宀	亣	古	宁	京	京		
1	2	3	4	5	6	7	8		

空 kōng

empty
spare time

空洞	kōng dòng	cavity; empty
空防	kōng fáng	air defence
空话	kōng huà	empty talk; idle talk
空欢喜	kōng huān xǐ	rejoice too soon
空间	kōng jiān	space
空军	kōng jūn	air force

The radical is 穴 (cave) - a space (宀) obtained by the removal or separation (八) of rock or earth. When a cave (穴) is excavated by labour (工) we have the character for empty: 空 . 空 also means at leisure or free from work.

`	八	宀	宀	穴	空	空	空			
1	2	3	4	5	6	7	8			

船 chuán

boat;
ship

船埠	chuán bù	wharf; quay
船壳	chuán ké	hull
船尾	chuán wěi	stern
船坞	chuán wù	dock; shipyard
船员	chuán yuán	(ship's) crew
船长	chuán zhǎng	captain; skipper
船只	chuán zhī	shipping; vessels

As a memory aid, 船 could refer to a boat (舟) with eight (八) survivors or mouths (口) - an allusion to Noah's Ark. The radical 舟 is a picture of a boat. The phonetic 㕣 probably means a coast; so 船 is a coastal (沿) vessel (舟). No matter how useful such a vessel is, "Like a thread without a needle, a boat is useless without water."

´	丿	刀	月	月	舟	舟	舟	船	船	船
1	2	3	4	5	6	7	8	9	10	11

贫 pín

poor

贫乏	pín fá	poor; short; lacking
贫寒	pín hán	poor;; poverty-stricken
贫困	pín kùn	poor; impoverished; in straitened circumstances
贫民	pín mín	poor people; pauper

The radical 貝 , a picture of cowrie, shells once used as money, represents wealth. 分 is to divide or scatter. So 贫 is to squander (分) one's wealth (貝) - to be poor. Even the poor cannot afford to ignore the warning: "If the poor associates with the rich, he will soon have no trousers to wear."

丿	八	分	分	分	贫	贫	贫			
1	2	3	4	5	6	7	8			

圆

yuán
round; dollar

圆规	yuán guī	compasses
圆滑	yuán huá	smooth and evasive; slick and sly
圆满	yuán mǎn	satisfactory
圆圈	yuán quān	circle; ring
圆舞曲	yuán wǔ qǔ	waltz
圆型	yuán xíng	circular; round

This character for round or dollar has undergone many changes since its original form: ○. The ideograph 員 meaning round (○) like a cowrie (貝), soon replaced it. Then it was altered to 圓, being reclarified and surrounded by 囗. Although hollowed out to 圆 the dollar is still changeable; it's easier to change dollars into goods than goods into dollars!

儿

ér
infant; child

儿歌	ér gē	children's song; nursery rhymes
儿科	ér kē	(department of) paediatrics
儿女	ér nǔ	sons and daughters; children

儿 is a pictograph of the growing child - from the crawling infant with open fontanels (○) to the little toddler (兒) with wobbly legs, now simplified to its present form: 儿. The loving care shown in the delineation of this character calls to mind the saying: "To understand your parents' love, raise your own children."

士

shì
scholar; gentleman

士兵	shì bīng	rank-and-file soldiers; privates
士女	shì nǔ	young men and women
士气	shì qì	morale
士绅	shì shēn	gentry
士卒	shì zú	soldiers; privates

According to this ideograph, a scholar or learned man (士) is a rarity: one (一) out of ten (十). He is also acquainted from one to ten, i.e., with all things. Scholars are a country's treasure, and with good reason: "It takes a tree ten years to grow up; it takes a century to educate man."

做 zuò
make;
produce

做东	zuò dōng	play the host
做法	zuò fǎ	way of doing or making a thing
做工	zuò gōng	do manual work; work
做鬼	zuò guǐ	play tricks; play an underhand game
做客	zuò kè	be a guest

sets forth man (亻) with a cause (故) to produce an effect. Hence The meaning: to make or produce. It also suggests man (亻) toiling 攵 until he gets old (古) sometimes for a fruitless cause. In the words of the proverb: "The hard work of a hundred years may be destroyed in an hour."

ノ	亻	亻	什	什	估	估	做	做	做	做
1	2	3	4	5	6	7	8	9	10	11

众 zhòng
crowd;
many

众多	zhòng duō	multitudinous; numerous
众人	zhòng rén	everybody
众望	zhòng wàng	people's expectations

The seal form 眾 shows three or many persons 川 as viewed by the eye 目 .Modified to 眔 , it was again altered to 众 - three persons, representing a crowd. It's easier to follow the crowd than to get the crowd to follow you. In the words of the proverb: "An army of a 1000 is easy to find; but, ah, how difficult to find a general!"

ノ	人	个	众	分	众
1	2	3	4	5	6

价 jià
pice;
value

估价	gū jià	estimate the value of; evaluate
讲价	jiǎng jià	bargain
价格	jià gé	price
价目	jià mù	marked price
价值	jià zhí	value worth

The ideograph for price (价) is derived by putting 亻 , man, the buyer against 贾 , the seller. 贾 , the seller, marks up the price to cover (西) his goods with value in cowries (贝). Paradoxically, the highest price you can pay for anything is to get it for nothing.

ノ	亻	亻	价	价	价
1	2	3	4	5	6

话 huà
speech; words

话别	huà bié	say a few parting words; say good-bye
话柄	huà bǐng	subject for ridicule
话旧	huà jiù	talk over old times; reminisce
话剧	huà jù	modern drama; stage play

話, meaning words or speech, is signified by words (言) of the tongue (舌).
講 meaning to speak or explain, is suggested by words (言) set in order (冓), 冓 being a graphic representation of the framework of a building. 講 is simplified to 讲. Sense is often linked with speech: "The full teapot makes no sound; the half-empty teapot makes much noise."

丶	讠	讠	讧	迂	话	话	话						
1	2	3	4	5	6	7	8						

语 yǔ
language

语词	yǔ cí	words and phrases
语调	yǔ diào	intonation
语法	yǔ fǎ	grammar
语汇	yǔ huì	vocabulary
语句	yǔ jù	sentence
语气	yǔ qì	tone; manner of speaking

吾, or five (五) mouths (口), stands for we, I, our or my. So our or my (吾) words (言) become language (語). Language is used in many ways. Some people use it to express thought, some to conceal thought, but most use it to replace thought.

丶	讠	讠	讧	迂	语	语	语	语					
1	2	3	4	5	6	7	8	9					

去 qù
go; leave

去处	qù chù	place to go; whereabouts
去垢剂	qù gòu jì	detergent
去路	qù lù	the way along which one is going; outlet
去年	qù nián	last year

去 is a pictograph of an empty vessel (厶) and its cover (土). The meaning "go" comes from the removal of the cover and contents of the vessel.
来, meaning "come", is a pictograph of growing wheat or barley, gratefully acknowledged as having come from the heavens above.

一	十	土	去	去									
1	2	3	4	5									

回 huí
return

回避	huí bì	evade; dodge
回驳	huí bó	refute
回程	huí chéng	return trip
回答	huí dá	answer; reply; response
回顾	huí gù	look back; review
回击	huí jī	return fire; counterattack

回 represents an eddy, like the curling clouds of smoke or whirlpools in water; or probably an object that rolls or turns on an axis; hence the idea of revolving or returning.

丨	冂	冋	冋	回	回
1	2	3	4	5	6

凸 tū
convex; protruding

凸窗	tū chuāng	bay window
凸轮	tū lún	cam
凸面镜	tū miàn jìng	convex mirror
凸透镜	tū tòu jìng	convex lens
凹面镜	āo miàn jìng	concave mirror
凹透镜	āo tòu jìng	concave lens
凹陷	āo xiàn	hollow; depressed

凸 to protrude, is graphically represented by the shape of this character. 凹 a hollow or dent, is another primitive character clearly indicated by its shape.

丨	ㄩ	㇄	凸	凸
1	2	3	4	5

丨	凵	凵	凹	凹
1	2	3	4	5

巢 cháo
nest

巢穴	cháo xué	den; lair
匪巢	feǐ cháo	bandits' lair
鸟巢	niǎo cháo	bird's nest

The seal from: 巢 depicts three fledglings in a nest on top of a tree. In the regular form: 巢 the birds remain,

but the nest is missing, displaced by fruit (果), though not for long, according to the saying: "If you upset a nest, you cannot expect to find any whole eggs underneath.

ㄑ	ㄍㄍ	ㄍㄍㄍ	巛	巛	巡	巡	単	単	巣	巢
1	2	3	4	5	6	7	8	9		

Appendix

Chinese Phonetic Alphabet (Hanyu Pinyin) and International Phonetic Alphabet

FINALS				INITIALS	
Hanyu Pinyin (Chinese Phonetic Alphabet)	International Phonetic Alphabet	Hanyu Pinyin (Chinese Phonetic Alphabet)	International Phonetic Alphabet	Hanyu Pinyin (Chinese Phonetic Alphabet)	International Phonetic Alphabet
i	i	ian	iæn	b	p
-i	ɿ	uan	uan	p	p′
-i	ʅ	üan	yan	m	m
u	u	en	ən	f	f
ü	y	in	in	d	t
er	ər	uen	uən	t	t′
a	a	ün	yn	n	n
ia	ia	ang	aŋ	l	l
ua	ua	iang	iaŋ	g	k
e	ɤ	uang	uaŋ	k	k′
o	o	eng	əŋ	h	x
uo	uo	ing	iŋ	j	tɕ
ie	iɛ	ong	uŋ	q	tɕ′
üe	yɛ	iong	yŋ	x	ɕ
ai	ai			zh	tʂ
uai	uai			ch	tʂ′
ei	ei			sh	ʂ
uei	uei			r	ʐ
ao	au			z	ts
iao	iau			c	ts′
ou	ou			s	s
iou	iou			y	j
an	an			w	w

Numbers

The Chinese count using the decimal system. Counting from 1 to 100 is as follows:

1	2	3	4	5	6	7	8	9	10
一	二	三	四	五	六	七	八	九	十
yī	èr	sān	sì	wǔ	liù	qī	bā	jiǔ	shí
十一 shí yī	→	→	→	→	→	→	→	→	二十 èr shí
二十一 èr shí yī	→	→	→	→	→	→	→	→	三十 sān shí
三十一 sān shí yī	→	→	→	→	→	→	→	→	四十 sì shí
四十一 sì shí yī	→	→	→	→	→	→	→	→	五十 wǔ shí
五十一 wú shí yī	→	→	→	→	→	→	→	→	六十 liù shí
六十一 liù shí yī	→	→	→	→	→	→	→	→	七十 qī shí
七十一 qī shí yī	→	→	→	→	→	→	→	→	八十 bā shí
八十一 bā shí yī	→	→	→	→	→	→	→	→	九十 jiǔ shí
九十一 jiǔ shí yī	→	→	→	→	→	→	→	→	一百 yī bǎi

Days and Months

Naming the months of a year in Chinese is simply done by using the appropriate number in front of the character for month (yue). So the months of the year are:

一月	yī yuè	January	七月	qī yuè	July
二月	èr yuè	February	八月	bā yuè	August
三月	sān yuè	March	九月	jiǔ yuè	September
四月	sì yuè	April	十月	shí yuè	October
五月	wǔ yuè	May	十一月	shí yi yuè	November
六月	liù yuè	June	十二月	shí èr yuè	December

Similarly, the days of the week, except Sunday, are indicated by adding one to six after the phrase 星期 (xingqi) so the names of Monday to Saturday in Chinese are:

星期一	xīngqī yī	Monday	星期四	xīngqī sì	Thursday
星期二	xīngqī èr	Tuesday	星期五	xīngqī wǔ	Friday
星期三	xīngqī sān	Wednesday	星期六	xīngqī liù	Saturday

However, you do not add seven to xingqi for Sunday in Chinese. Instead, you add 日 ri, the character for day after xingqi.